GACE

Business

Education

Exam

"You never fail until you stop trying" - Albert Einstein

For inquiries;
info@xmprep.com

GACE Business Education Exam #1

Test Taking Tips

☐ Take a deep breath and relax

☐ Read directions carefully

☐ Read the questions thoroughly

☐ Make sure you understand what is being asked

☐ Go over all of the choices before you answer

☐ Paraphrase the question

☐ Eliminate the options you know are wrong

☐ Check your work

☐ Think positively and do your best

Table of Contents

TEST DIRECTION

DIRECTIONS

Read the questions carefully and then choose the ONE best answer to each question.

Be sure to allocate your time carefully so you are able to complete the entire test within the testing session. You may go back and review your answers at any time.

You may use any available space in your test booklet for scratch work.

Questions in this booklet are not actual test questions but they are the samples for commonly asked questions.

This test aims to cover all topics which may appear on the actual test. However some topics may not be covered.

Studying this booklet will be preparing you for the actual test. It will not guarantee improving your test score but it will help you pass your exam on the first attempt.

Some useful tips for answering multiple choice questions;

- Start with the questions that you can easily answer.

- Underline the keywords in the question.

- Be sure to read all the choices given.

- Watch for keywords such as NOT, always, only, all, never, completely.

- Do not forget to answer every question.

1

Which of the following should happen before carrying out any management functions?

A) Processing
B) Brainstorming
C) Analyzing
D) Planning

2

A company orders large amounts of bolts and washers, thus, it negotiates with the vendor to have an additional five percent off the total invoice.

Which of the following is the business negotiating?

A) A cash rebate
B) Delivery terms
C) A quantity discount
D) Service terms

3

Which of the following actions must a business take to significantly impact long-term employee productivity?

A) Increase the production quotas
B) Raise performance expectations
C) Conduct effective employee evaluations
D) Implement a pushing management style

4

Which of the following refers to the process of planning activities in advance, setting priorities, and avoiding nonproductive diversions?

A) Time management
B) Productivity
C) Natural ability
D) Accountability

5

Which of the following do companies collect and analyze to come up with decisions that would be best for the company?

A) Information
B) Markets
C) Demand
D) Ratings

6

A **special order** is a request for a particular product or one that a seller usually does not have it in stock.

Which of the following is an example of an item that most likely requires a retailer to place a special order with its manufacturer?

A) A color ink cartridge for a computer printer

B) Blinds for a nonstandard-size window

C) Windshield wipers for a 2008 Honda Accord

D) A cellphone charger for a popular smartphone

7

It is common that there is an increase in sales during the holiday season. Thus, a company manager decided to hire two extra part-time employees.

Which of the following would happen if there is no increase in sales?

A) There would be business expansion.

B) The business would lose income.

C) There would be additional profit.

D) The business may file bankruptcy.

8

The local government requires manufacturing companies to dispose of their waste safely and correctly. To do this, they design waste disposal processes to comply with the regulations.

Which of the following factors affecting the business process design, is the situation given above an example of?

A) Natural

B) Technological

C) Regulatory

D) Human

9

An **investment** is an asset purchased with the concept that it will give an income in the future or it may be sold at a higher price for a profit.

Which of the following is the best age to begin investing if you are 16 in the present?

A) 16

B) 18

C) 21

D) 25

10

Budget need to be flexible since it is only an estimation.

Which of the following may cause a business to adjust its budget figures?

A) Operating policies
B) Economic trends
C) Sales procedures
D) Local elections

11

Which of the following does a manager need to do if his/her team members cannot reach a resolution by themselves?

A) Negotiate with external sources.
B) Help in resolving the conflict.
C) Change the scope of the project.
D) Evaluate the reward system.

12

Job searching is the act of looking for employment for reasons such as unemployment, underemployment, discontentment with the current, or a desire for new and better opportunities.

Which of the following is the first step in conducting a job search?

A) Completion of applications
B) Scheduling of interviews
C) Identifying any leads in job searching
D) Contacting or reaching out to the employers

13

In what phase of a project are the release of equipment, materials, and team members completed?

A) Closing
B) Planning
C) Initiating
D) Scheduling

14

What type of inventory system is designed for recording the actual cost associated with the inventory through a physical count?

A) The perpetual inventory system
B) The temporary inventory system
C) The just-in-time inventory system
D) The periodic system

15

When a borrower agrees to a loan, he/she makes a contractual agreement to repay the loan in a particular manner within a specific period.

Who is legally entitled to repay a bank loan if the loan borrower fails to make payments as indicated in the loan contract?

A) Debt collectors
B) Credit union
C) Treasury Department
D) Cosigner

16

Limited liability is a type of liability wherein an individual's liability is limited to a fixed sum, typically the amount invested in a partnership or company.

What form of business ownership does limited liability belong to?

A) Joint proprietorship
B) Corporation
C) Partnership
D) Sole proprietorship

17

Inventory consists of the raw materials and products that are work-in-progress as well as finished goods.

Which of the following can result in running out of inventory?

A) Low demand
B) More satisfied customers
C) Higher productivity
D) Higher taxes

18

Knowledge management involves the use of the expertise, idea, and information of resources, that may be internal or external, to help an organization to accomplish its goals.

Which of the following is an ethical issue that relates to knowledge management in the workplace?

A) An employee does not share a critical information with the management which may help them achieve its goals.
B) The president of a small company asks the opinion of her/his executive team regarding a business decision.
C) A project leader orders each member of his/her team to give a status report to the group.
D) A sales manager shares with his/her sales staff the firm's quarterly sales goals.

19

A **trade secret** is anything not generally known that make a business obtain an advantage over competitors or customers.

Which of the following hinders the ability to maintain trade secrets of a company?

A) Reverse engineering
B) Copyright reform initiatives
C) Systematic neutralizing
D) Process fragmentation

20

Which step in a business process will indicate if there is an improvement in the quality?

A) Implementation
B) Documentation
C) Evaluation
D) Recommendation

21

A **marketing concept** states a business' need to analyze and meet the customer's need better than their competitors.

In implementing the marketing concept, which of the following role does the utility have?

A) A delivery process
B) A payment method
C) A satisfaction gauge
D) A cost-saving tool

22

What position do a department manager, a small business manager, and regional manager belong to?

A) General management
B) Operations management
C) Supply chain management
D) Business analytics

23

The transformation of a range of inputs into outputs which are demanded by the market is the concern of a production process.

Which of the following would production processes that significantly rely on expensive equipment and materials be classified?

A) Labor-intensive
B) Standardized
C) Capital-intensive
D) Intermittent

24

Resources coming from the environment that can be utilized by consumers are called **natural resources**.

Which of the following situations illustrates a search for an alternative limited natural resource?

A) Looking for oil on the ocean floor
B) Buying oil for a higher price
C) Replacement of oil with natural gas
D) Conservation of the oil utilized

25

Maintenance involves activities that are required to be done to maintain an asset's original condition while being subjected to normal wear and tear.

Which of the following is an advantage for a business of a good maintenance program?

A) Emergency repairs will be needed more often.

B) Fixed costs are increased.

C) Customers are more likely to be satisfied.

D) Maintenance costs can be added to profits.

26

Project planning consists of a procedural step in project management. This is where all the documentation required is created to assure the completion of a project.

Which of the following is a useful communication strategy in project planning?

A) The team members are grouped according to the type and level of information.

B) Identifying the possible costs for the project.

C) Assigning responsibility to meet quality requirements.

D) Assessing the possible duration of completion for each deliverable.

27

Just in time (JIT) inventory is a management system wherein the production of materials is dependent on the required demands.

How does technology impact just-in-time inventory management?

A) Eliminates the need for supplier relationships.

B) Causes a disruption in the supply chain.

C) Allows inventory to be regularly monitored.

D) Increases the cost of warehouse storage.

28

Mr. Jenkins is the sole owner of a small boat rental company but eventually invited his friend to join him. However, he is concerned with the cost associated with changes in the organization.

Which of the following is the best action for Mr. Jenkins to take?

A) Change the business into a partnership

B) Change the business into a joint venture

C) Change the business into a cooperative

D) Change the business into a corporation

CONTINUE ▶

29

If a small business owner wishes to use software to manage the business' finances, which of the following products would he or she typically use?

A) Spreadsheet
B) Knowledge management utility
C) Double-entry accounting software
D) Relational database

31

A job opening refers to a job vacancy; thus a business wants to hire an individual for a particular job.

However, is it appropriate for a job seeker to send a letter of application to a business not advertising a job opening?

A) Yes, he/she should write to each business in the industry.
B) No, a letter is applicable only as a response to job advertisements.
C) No, the business will dismiss the letter if there are no job openings.
D) Yes, he/she can write if he/she has learned about a job opening.

30

The **Perfect Competition** is a market structure consisting of a large number of buyers and sellers all engaged in the buying and selling of similar products at a single price.

Which of the following is a characteristic of a perfectly competitive market structure?

A) There are fewer restrictions thus new suppliers can freely enter the market.
B) The decisions of a few large suppliers primarily determine the price.
C) The decision of the suppliers regarding the production and price are based on the possible reactions of their competitors.
D) Other than the price, the output of each supplier can be distinguished from one another.

32

Tacit knowledge is the knowledge composed of personal opinions, experiences, expertise, or understanding that cannot be easily articulated, stored, or quantified.

Which of the following techniques is used to capture tacit knowledge that involves gathering a group of people together to talk about how they execute their work, the challenges they face, and how they overcome it?

A) Parliamentary procedure
B) Channeling discussion
C) Critical interaction
D) Repetitious feedback

33

Tacit knowledge is an explicit knowledge that is difficult to transfer to another person by means of writing it. You get it from personal experience, it is not written in the books and etc.

Which of the following software program enables many employees to access and share information, including tacit knowledge?

A) Presentation

B) Groupware

C) Spreadsheet

D) Recovery

34

Which of the following research techniques is the most appropriate, if a marketing department of a small business wants to gather data on how and why a product continuously succeed after many years?

A) Organize focus groups

B) Request user surveys

C) Gather reviews by experts

D) Conduct one-on-one or personal interviews

35

Control activities are the actions based on policies and procedures that help assure that the management's response to mitigate risks are carried out.

What control activity does a project manager perform if his/her team completed the software-development phase of the project seven days ahead of schedule?

A) Assessing a setback

B) Evaluating a time constraint

C) Changing a process

D) Tracking a milestone

36

Economic risk is the possibility of an investment to be affected by the government regulation, political stability, or exchange rates. This commonly occurs in a foreign country.

Which of the following can the government laws and regulations result in an economic risk?

A) It reduces the profit of a business.

B) It can cause environmental problems.

C) It can make businesses less secure.

D) It can protect the consumers.

37

Six Sigma is a quality-management framework that involves the continuous setting of higher goals to achieve. It is based on previous goals to set higher goals for continuous improvement of the quality of the business's goods, services, or processes.

Which of the following is the other overall purpose of the Six Sigma quality-management framework aside from satisfying customers?

A) Improving technology

B) Lowering the costs

C) Simplifying activities

D) Identifying needs

38

A **follow-up survey** is a type of survey wherein the households involved are repeatedly interviewed to obtain information on important events.

Which of the following is the most important to communicate with the survey recipients when sending a follow-up survey upon buying a product?

A) The number of consumers that the survey is sent with.

B) The objective of the survey and how the results will be utilized.

C) The process involve in selecting the recipient of the survey.

D) The importance of carefully following instructions.

39

A **project** is a task that will require a lot of time and effort to finish.

Which of the following is correct about projects?

A) Projects produce goods, not services.

B) In a project, process is more crucial than its results.

C) Projects are short-term undertakings.

D) Projects rely on traditional management structures.

40

A **Work Breakdown Structure (WBS)** is utilized for breaking down a project into manageable sections.

Which of the following is the main benefit of developing a work breakdown structure in managing large projects?

A) Lessens the demand to manage each task

B) Lessens the need for setting project milestones

C) Prevents work repetition

D) Removes unforeseen circumstances

41

Trade theory involves analysis of patterns of international trade, its origin as well as its implications on the welfare.

Which of the following are not one of the four main idealized market structures used in trade theory?

A) Perfect monopoly

B) Monopoly

C) Perfect competition

D) Monopolistic competition

42

Business analysis is the process of investigating and evaluating a business issue, problem, method, or approach.

Which of the following is involved when employees review and analyze financial reports and income data from different time frames?

A) Influencing the opinion of others

B) Providing evidence

C) Informing of customers

D) Data comparison

43

Which of the following is the main priority of an employee?

A) Preparing a purchase order that needs to be faxed to the seller within two days.

B) Making reservations at a restaurant for a business luncheon scheduled to be held in two weeks.

C) Copyinga three-page document for a meeting with a customer scheduled five hours from now.

D) Completing a status report that takes 45 minutes to do for a meeting that will occur in an hour.

44

Supply chain management involves the supervision of the process of getting products into the marketplace and managing the flow of goods.

Which of the following is a goal of effective supply chain management?

A) Reducing the inventory

B) Management of customer relations

C) Planning strategies for promotion

D) Keeping marketing data

45

A marketable item that is manufactured to satisfy the wants and needs of the consumers is reffered to as a **commodity**.

Which of the following can result from a limited commodity?

A) Cost-push inflation
B) Demand-pull inflation
C) Hyperinflation
D) Price stability

46

Project management software helps project managers collaborate in task distribution, time tracking, budgeting, resource planning, team collaboration and meet goals on time.

Which of the following ability does a project-management software lack?

A) Generating reports
B) Tracking resources
C) Finding input errors
D) Sorting data

47

At a factory outlet store, some of the incoming merchandise is unpacked by receiving clerks, while some are left sealed for inventory clerks or salespeople to unpack and arrange for display which results in confusion.

Which of the following should the human resources department do to solve the problem?

A) New workers must be hired and trained for the receiving department.
B) Create a job description and conduct job function analyses.
C) Discuss with the workers their job responsibilities.
D) Forecast the future labor needs of the receiving department

48

A sports lover wants to start his own business focusing on sporting goods. However, he has a minimal time for the day-to-day operations of the business.

Which of the following would be applicable for such cases?

A) Corporation
B) General partnership
C) Sole proprietorship
D) Close corporation

49

A **proactive management** involves managing a business using strategies that addresses which of the following?

A) Prevention of risks

B) Advance planning for a change

C) Creating long-term plans only

D) Encouragement of individualism

50

Raw materials are the resources used by businesses for the production of its finished goods. They usually maintain an inventory of materials they use to produce their products.

Which of the following raw materials might a business keep on hand for production?

A) Grain, minerals, leather, and oil

B) Oil, grain, shoes, and household cleanser

C) Leather, bolts, stapler, and ore

D) Minerals, tables, leather, and paper

51

Customer situation involves dealing with the needs of the customers for their satisfaction.

Which of the following benefits can an employee gain if he/she solved difficult customer situations?

A) Difficult customers are encountered less frequently.

B) A salary increase will automatically be given by the company's head.

C) The customers will be happier.

D) Valuable communication skills are gained.

52

Which of the following do managers possess if they can understand how all of the functions of the company are interrelated with each other?

A) Innovative ideas

B) Technical competence

C) Conceptual skills

D) Interpersonal skills

53

Companies face **internal risks** which are within the organization and arise during normal operation. **External risks,** on the other hand, result from economic events that arise outside of a company's organization.

Which of the following is the importance of choosing a risk measure for internal and external risk?

A) It assigns the audience getting the resulting financial reports.

B) It defines the maximum number of clients that a financial institution can serve effectively.

C) It defines the minimum reserve requirements needed in financial trading.

D) It recognizes the types of risks that will be encountered by a financial institution.

54

Human resources need to engage in strategic planning to meet the company's mission concerning the workforce.

Which of the following is correct about human resources needs?

A) Human resources needs are always changing.

B) Human resources needs are difficult to meet in high-tech industries.

C) Human resources needs have no way to determine when the change will happen.

D) Human resources needs are the same for every business.

Revenue/ Expenses	Amount
Car Repair Revenue	$4,120
Car Wash Revenue	$6,523
Advertising Expense	$875
Maintenance Expense	$1,245
Rent Expense	$3,200
Utilities Expense	$950

Use the information in the table regarding Asphalt's Auto Repair Shop and Car Wash for the month of February.

Which of the following percentages represents the return on sales for the month of February?

A) 41%

B) 63%

C) 59%

D) 37%

Cash Flow Ratio is a measure of how well a company can pay off its current liabilities. A higher ratio reflects the firm's financial ability to pay its debts.

Investors often calculate the price-to-cash flow ratio (P/CF) of potential investments to compare their relative worth.

Sky Reach
Current Stock Price: $14.36
Cash Flow per Share: $5.21

Flying Fair
Current Stock Price: $22.78
Cash Flow per Share: $4.12

Beyond the Clouds
Current Stock Price: $18.50
Cash Flow per Share: $3.59

Clash on Cloud
Current Stock Price: $25.81
Cash Flow per Share: $6.94

Which of the following airlines given above is most likely to be undervalued using its price-to-cash flow ratio as the basis?

A) Clash on Cloud

B) Beyond the Clouds

C) Sky Reach

D) Flying Fair

57

How does Small Business Association (SBA) aid entrepreneurs who are starting a business through guaranty loan program?

A) Implementing truth-in-lending laws and anti-discriminatory practices when private lenders give loans to entrepreneurs.

B) Restricting the amount of interest the private lenders may charge on the entrepreneurs starting a new business.

C) Provide a government-funded pool of money wherein the entrepreneurs can draw.

D) Shouldering most of the risk for the loans made by private lenders for them to be more willing in loaning money to entrepreneurs.

58

Lucas, a business-minded college student, aspires to start a business. However, he does not have enough capital to start but believes he can obtain it through an **initial public offering (IPO)**.

Which of the following category does IPO belong?

A) Income
B) Equity
C) Asset
D) Debt

59

Entrepreneurial Ventures focuses on giving advisory services to companies at early and mid-stage.

Which of the following is an example of an entrepreneurial venture?

A) A bakery creates a "cretzel," a cross-over between a crescent and a pretzel, as a new product.

B) A pumpkin farm offers pumpkin carving and costume contests to stir more interest.

C) A juice bar decides to purchase trucks to sell juice on site during special events.

D) A veterinarian invents and sells a device that prevents horse water troughs from freezing.

60

A young entrepreneur used her entire income to purchase two goods, namely A and B.

What should she best do when her income and the price of goods A & B are doubled?

A) Purchase twice of each good.
B) Buy more of good A and less of good B.
C) Buy less of both goods.
D) Buy equal amounts of goods A and B.

SECTION 1 MANAGEMENT & ENTREPRENEURSHIP

#	Answer	Topic	Subtopic	#	Answer	Topic	Subtopic	#	Answer	Topic	Subtopic	#	Answer	Topic	Subtopic
1	D	TB	SB3	16	B	TA	SA7	31	D	TB	SB3	46	C	TB	SB3
2	C	TB	SB3	17	A	TB	SB3	32	B	TB	SB3	47	B	TB	SB3
3	C	TB	SB3	18	A	TB	SB3	33	B	TB	SB3	48	A	TA	SA7
4	A	TB	SB3	19	A	TB	SB3	34	B	TA	SA7	49	B	TB	SB3
5	A	TB	SB3	20	C	TB	SB3	35	D	TB	SB3	50	A	TB	SB3
6	B	TB	SB3	21	C	TB	SB3	36	A	TB	SB3	51	D	TB	SB3
7	B	TB	SB3	22	A	TB	SB3	37	B	TB	SB3	52	C	TB	SB3
8	C	TB	SB3	23	C	TB	SB3	38	B	TB	SB3	53	C	TB	SB3
9	A	TA	SA7	24	A	TB	SB3	39	C	TB	SB3	54	A	TA	SA4
10	B	TB	SB3	25	C	TB	SB3	40	C	TB	SB3	55	A	TB	SB3
11	B	TB	SB3	26	A	TB	SB3	41	A	TB	SB3	56	C	TB	SB3
12	C	TB	SB3	27	C	TB	SB3	42	D	TB	SB3	57	D	TA	SA7
13	A	TB	SB3	28	A	TA	SA7	43	D	TB	SB3	58	B	TA	SA7
14	A	TB	SB3	29	C	TA	SA7	44	A	TB	SB3	59	D	TA	SA7
15	D	TB	SB3	30	A	TB	SB3	45	A	TB	SB3	60	D	TA	SA7

Topics & Subtopics

Code	Description	Code	Description
SA4	Career Development	TA	Business Evironment
SA7	Entrepreneurship	TB	Business Basics
SB3	Business Management		

TEST DIRECTION

DIRECTIONS

Read the questions carefully and then choose the ONE best answer to each question.

Be sure to allocate your time carefully so you are able to complete the entire test within the testing session. You may go back and review your answers at any time.

You may use any available space in your test booklet for scratch work.

Questions in this booklet are not actual test questions but they are the samples for commonly asked questions.

This test aims to cover all topics which may appear on the actual test. However some topics may not be covered.

Studying this booklet will be preparing you for the actual test. It will not guarantee improving your test score but it will help you pass your exam on the first attempt.

Some useful tips for answering multiple choice questions;

- Start with the questions that you can easily answer.

- Underline the keywords in the question.

- Be sure to read all the choices given.

- Watch for keywords such as NOT, always, only, all, never, completely.

- Do not forget to answer every question.

1

Which of the following is a type of communication employed by the company's president if he/she wants to inform all the employees regarding the change in insurance coverage?

A) Lateral communication
B) Staff communication
C) Upward communication
D) Informal communication

2

A business teacher is designing a unit to make her students engage in an extended project.

Which of the following should she do to connect learning and work?

A) A work-study job
B) A job-training membership
C) A field-based investigation
D) A job-shadowing opportunity

3

It is crucial to ask for suggestions when proposing assigned tasks to a team.

Which of the following is the result of asking for feedback?

A) Promoting authority
B) Establishing openness
C) Setting expected outcomes
D) Discouraging over-reporting

4

To create a positive relationship with the customers, employees tend to offer something to the customers, but they have to live up to the terms of the commitment.

Which of the following characteristics does an employee exhibit on the situation above?

A) Assertiveness
B) Sociability
C) Creativity
D) Dependability

5

Upward communication involves the transfer of messages to individuals at a higher position in the business.

Which of the following type of information is often transmitted through upward communication?

A) Instructions
B) Corrections
C) Suggestions
D) Evaluations

A **persuasive letter** is a letter that is written with the intention of persuading an organization/s or individual/s into accepting the interest or perspective of the sender.

Which of the following is the importance of inserting logical evidence in a persuasive letter for businesses?

A) To explain the sender's idea using a strong language.
B) To pressure response from the recipient.
C) To show information that is interesting.
D) To present the message more convincingly.

If a salesperson perceives a situation the same as what the customer views it, she exhibits which of the following?

A) Tolerance
B) Empathy
C) Cooperation
D) Responsibility

Communication involves sending and receiving of information between two or more people. The sender is the person responsible for sending the message while the person that receives the information is referred to as the receiver.

Which type of information is usually not conveyed during communication?

A) Attitude
B) Emotions
C) Private thoughts
D) Beliefs

The **emerging market economy** refers to the advancement of a nation's economy typically through accelerated growth and industrialization.

Which of the following foreign investors usually tend to do when there is a decline in the emerging market economy?

A) Pay lower for each transaction.
B) Immediately withdraw the money from the emerging market.
C) Use the situation as an opportunity to invest more.
D) Aid in the recovery of the emerging market.

CONTINUE ▶

10

A **persuasive essay** is an essay constructed to get the reader to agree with the writer's point of view. In her persuasive paper, Mary starts by stating the dilemma at hand and then explains the answer that she believes will solve the dilemma.

Which of the following is Mary using in organizing the information?

A) Problem/Solution

B) Alphabetical

C) Chronological

D) Deductive

11

To build long-term relationships with their clients, which of the following should finance professionals do?

A) Require a short-term contract to be signed by clients.

B) Be honest, open, and trustworthy.

C) Do a client follow-up every two years.

D) Invest all clients' money conservatively.

12

Anna is assigned on reminding her co-employees to complete and sign their time sheets before leaving for home every weekend.

Which of the following is the most appropriate communication channel to be used for routine workplace messages similar to Anna's case above?

A) Phone

B) Letter

C) Fax

D) Email

13

Businesses are required by the government to give specific financial information to regulatory agencies and shareholders.

Which of the following is a financial data that can be asked from businesses by the government or regulatory agencies?

A) Complex memorandum

B) Accounting portfolio

C) Annual report

D) Informal monthly contract

14

A new business leader wants to promote the need for the business to comply with safety requirements and procedures.

What should the leader do to solicit greater staff support regarding his goal?

A) Conduct periodic safety inspections and share the results with everyone.

B) Implement more strict and severe disciplinary actions for noncompliance violations.

C) Share with the staff research-based information about the safety problems in the business.

D) Remind everyone through emails regarding the needs for business safety.

15

Which of the following refers to the activity of electronically buying or selling of products on online services or over the Internet?

A) Market economy

B) Foreign exchange

C) E-commerce

D) Electronic signature

16

Asking relevant questions about the job at the end of an interview is part of having a well-conversed interview.

If Andrew, an aspiring applicant, will be having an interview with a car business company, which of the following should Andrew do to be prepared for the questions of the interview?

A) Rely on the interviewer to come up with the questions.

B) Consult with others about what questions should be asked.

C) Research the company's background before the interview.

D) Investigate the interviewer's high school background and ask about it to form a personal relationship.

17

In business, the simplest business type is the **sole proprietorship** by which a person can operate a business being responsible for its debts.

Which of the following options is not true regarding sole proprietorship?

A) It can quickly adapt to change because one person operates it.

B) In the US, the sole proprietorship is the most common form of business organization.

C) It is easy to dissolve the business because a single owner can quickly make the decision.

D) It is a legal entity, and there is no distinction between the business and the owner.

18

Which of the following would risk business in losing its good reputation?

A) Encouraging employees to report behaviors that are questionable.

B) Use of tactics that are questionable to gain profitability.

C) Demand credit information from the new suppliers.

D) Give accurate information to the stockholders.

19

A business leader wants to use hierarchical communication in his company.

Which of the following is true about business leader's communication if he first relays the information to the department chairs then to the grade-level team leaders and lastly to the team members?

A) It is consistent with his intention.

B) It is inconsistent with his intention.

C) It is clearer than his intention.

D) It has higher impact than his intention.

20

While preparing a business presentation, which of the following approaches is the most appropriate to use?

A) Concluding the presentation with a Q & A period.

B) Establishing the presenter's credibility at the start of the presentation.

C) Incorporating the objectives at the end of the presentation.

D) Using the supporting materials in the presentation.

21

Within a country's borders, the goods and services produced in a specific period have a monetary value called the **gross domestic product (GDP)**.

Which of the following are used for some figures in calculating GDP?

A) Predictions
B) Estimates
C) Forecasts
D) Transfers

22

Why is it necessary for a speaker to make eye contact with the members of the audience?

A) It establishes the speaker's confidence about the material she is explaining to the audience.
B) It tells the audience that the speaker is dishonest.
C) It creates a bond of distrust.
D) It results in the audience to be less likely engaged in the discussion.

23

The International Organization for Standardization (ISO) is a non-governmental international organization that develops and publishes standards to facilitate the coordination and unification of industrial standards.

Which of the following is not correct about ISO?

A) ISO defines global measures about the quality of individual products.
B) The common name given to quality management standards is ISO 9000
C) ISO 14000 standards monitor and control the effects of business activities of the companies on the environment.
D) ISO was founded on 23 February 1971, headquartered in Geneva, Switzerland, and works in 162 countries.

24

A **business letter** is a formal document that is usually between companies, or with a customer, client or other external parties.

After the inside address, which of the following part of a business letter follows?

A) Salutation
B) Dateline
C) Signature line
D) Body

CONTINUE ▶

25

Among the given list of policies, which of the following actions would most likely increase foreign trade?

A) Establishing free-trade zones
B) Applying specific tariffs
C) Implementing ad valorem tariffs
D) Employing packaging regulations

26

Customer feedback is crucial because it gives the business owners an idea on how to improve their business, product, or service to the customers.

Which of the following is an indication of a positive result from the proper handling of customer complaints?

A) Increase markdowns
B) Foster objections
C) Promote goodwill
D) Increase returns

27

Transparency, as used in business, is operating in such a way that it is easy for others to see and understand what actions are being performed.

The principles of transparency are best illustrated by which of the situations below?

A) A due process procedure is strictly followed in disciplining an issue.
B) Reports on the status of the business budget are regularly submitted to the business leader.
C) A variety of stakeholders are recruited to create the vision and mission of the business.
D) Decisions in eliminating or adjusting funding are justified with data and reasonable explanations.

28

Which of the following is the most important reason in maintaining a database of building maintenance and repairing records of a business?

A) For identifying approved vendors when there are purchases required.
B) For promoting effective organizational management.
C) For preventing emergency repairs from occurring within the facility.
D) For encouraging the staff to have a more efficient energy consumption.

29

A **global supply chain** is a network that is created among different worldwide companies that produce, handle, and distribute products.

Which of the following is a strategy to help manage risks in a global supply chain?

A) Only hire local workers.

B) Work within the same time zone only.

C) Allow lower quality levels.

D) Work with experienced partners abroad.

30

Which of the following is essential for building trust, respect, and a mutually beneficial partnership that is, in turn, will help in creating a long-term business relationship?

A) Ongoing communication

B) Rigid policies

C) Flexible lead times

D) Autocratic management

31

Excellence is what you strive for when you believe in what you are doing and that the value of what you do warrants the persistent commitment to its betterment.

Which of the following should a business leader demonstrate to show the best means of communicating a commitment to excellence?

A) Model high expectations for self and others in the business.

B) Set new high goals to achieve for all staff.

C) Create detailed instructions to specify roles of staff.

D) Allow staff to make their own decisions for improvement based on their assessment.

32

An **analytical report** involves examination of a problem or an issue as well as the recommended action to solve them.

Which of the following should analytical report writers use to support the information that the readers disagree?

A) Personal opinions

B) Logical arguments

C) Enthusiastic statements

D) Technical statistics

33

Which of the following demonstrates that business activities are interrelated?

A) Business advertisements need to adjust if a new product is introduced.

B) The others must adjust in response to a change in the business' activity.

C) As businesses change its goals, its strategies and tactics change as well.

D) When a business manager is promoted as vice president, her department needs to adjust to the change.

34

Globalization arises from the interchange of products or ideas of businesses from domestic and national markets with the other markets around the globe.

Which of the following could have caused an acceleration in the globalization of financial markets?

A) The shift towards the fixed exchange rates

B) The development of practices in protectionism

C) A decline in the access of foreign markets to domestic markets

D) A decrease in the regulations of the government

35

Customer relations refer to the way a business communicates and interacts with the customers to attain long-term relationship.

How do businesses make use of technology to build positive customer relations?

A) Constructing targeted marketing campaigns

B) Placing pop-up advertisements on websites

C) Sending of unsolicited e-mails

D) Contacting customers at home

36

Communication is exchanging information by speaking, writing, or using some other medium.

Which of the following is not correct about communication?

A) Nonverbal communication is the use of body movements to send a message.

B) Communication is the exchange of information by speaking, writing, or using some other medium.

C) Using obscene language in a speech is inappropriate.

D) Pitch has a psychological effect that influences how people perceive your speech's content.

The government has approved a budget to increase infrastructure, public transportation, education, health care, and housing.

Which of the following could be the short-term effect of this budget on the nation's economy?

A) Inflation will remain stable or gradually increase.

B) Job growth will decrease or remain unstable.

C) Business failures and bankruptcies will increase.

D) Gross domestic product (GDP) will increase.

In order to introduce a new line of hair care products to many other countries, a U.S. cosmetics manufacturer plans to start a marketing campaign.

Which of the following will ensure that the campaign be consistent with the cultural values and beliefs of the target countries?

A) Employ focus groups consisting of the targeted parts of the indigenous populations for testing the marketing themes.

B) Examine the success of similar marketing themes among different ethnic groups in the U.S. market.

C) In order to identify areas of cultural bias, ask the bilingual staff of the company to review the marketing themes.

D) Use a variety of alternative marketing themes in marketing the product in several cities per country.

39

Scottish people are known for being warm and friendly.

If an American businessman wants to close a deal with a Scottish businessman, does he/she need to change his/her communication style to adapt to the Scottish culture?

A) No, since Western and Scottish cultures tend to share similar qualities.

B) Yes, this is to prevent any unnecessary action that may be offensive to the Scottish culture.

C) Yes, since for many reasons, Scottish tend to dislike Americans thus he/she needs to be careful with his/her actions.

D) No, he/she does not have to do anything special for the trip since Scottish people speak English.

40

What should a company do when there is a change in the existing contact information of a customer?

A) Enter the contact information of the customer in a new database .

B) Place the customer's information in the employee directory.

C) Make a new record containing the changes in the customer's information.

D) Update the record of the customer in the company's database.

41

A disagreement between the workers, with three of them agreeing on one view while the other two expressing their opposition to a specific business issue has already become an impasse.

Which of the following is the best thing that a business leader can do to achieve consensus among his workers?

A) Point out the essential ideas about the opposing views and use them to make an alternative option.

B) Support the majority view and dismiss the minority's ideas.

C) Be neutral about facilitating the discussion while encouraging both groups to identify common ground.

D) Clarify to both groups that the decision should be in the best interest of the business.

42

Hierarchy is a way of structuring an organization by utilizing different levels of authority and a vertical link, or chain of command, between superior and subordinate levels of the organization.

In a hierarchical organization, which of the following is the best explanation of general communication?

A) In a hierarchical organization, the flow of communication is not distinct.

B) Orders and information for decision making flow towards the lower levels in the hierarchy.

C) Orders and information for decision making flows towards the higher levels in the hierarchy.

D) Orders flow down the levels of the hierarchy while information for decision making flows up.

43

If a country increases its demands for imports over domestically produced goods, the international value of its coin and exports will change in which of the following ways?

A) The international value of the coin would appreciate, exports would decline.

B) The international value of the coin would appreciate, exports would increase.

C) The international value of the coin would depreciate, exports would decline.

D) The international value of the coin would depreciate, exports would increase.

Adaptability is an essential organizational attribute wherein an individual can recognize the need to change based on the current and future changes in the environment.

Which of the following management practices is the most appropriate for promoting adaptability in a global business environment?

A) Launching sales initiatives to conform to the corporate calendar

B) Changing strategies to accommodate local conditions

C) Developing a set of fixed responses to anticipated problems

D) Launching sales initiatives to conform to the corporate calendar

SECTION 2 COMMUNICATION & INTL BUSINESS

#	Answer	Topic	Subtopic	#	Answer	Topic	Subtopic	#	Answer	Topic	Subtopic	#	Answer	Topic	Subtopic
1	B	TA	S2	12	D	TA	S2	23	D	TA	S2	34	D	TA	S6
2	C	TA	S2	13	C	TA	S6	24	A	TA	S2	35	A	TA	S2
3	B	TA	S2	14	A	TA	S2	25	A	TA	S6	36	D	TA	S2
4	D	TA	S2	15	C	TA	S6	26	C	TA	S2	37	D	TA	S6
5	C	TA	S2	16	C	TA	S2	27	D	TA	S2	38	A	TA	S6
6	D	TA	S2	17	D	TA	S2	28	B	TA	S2	39	B	TA	S2
7	B	TA	S2	18	B	TA	S2	29	D	TA	S6	40	D	TA	S2
8	C	TA	S2	19	B	TA	S2	30	A	TA	S2	41	C	TA	S2
9	B	TA	S6	20	B	TA	S2	31	A	TA	S2	42	D	TA	S2
10	A	TA	S2	21	B	TA	S6	32	B	TA	S2	43	D	TA	S6
11	B	TA	S2	22	A	TA	S2	33	B	TA	S6	44	B	TA	S6

Topics & Subtopics

Code	Description	Code	Description
SA2	Business Communication	TA	Business Evironment
SA6	International Business		

CONTINUE ▶

TEST DIRECTION

Read the questions carefully and then choose the ONE best answer to each question.

Be sure to allocate your time carefully so you are able to complete the entire test within the testing session. You may go back and review your answers at any time.

You may use any available space in your test booklet for scratch work.

Questions in this booklet are not actual test questions but they are the samples for commonly asked questions.

This test aims to cover all topics which may appear on the actual test. However some topics may not be covered.

Studying this booklet will be preparing you for the actual test. It will not guarantee improving your test score but it will help you pass your exam on the first attempt.

Some useful tips for answering multiple choice questions;

- Start with the questions that you can easily answer.

- Underline the keywords in the question.

- Be sure to read all the choices given.

- Watch for keywords such as NOT, always, only, all, never, completely.

- Do not forget to answer every question.

1

In the context of taxation as well as the international business operations of a company in its residence and source state, which of the following is true?

A) The residence state mitigates the tax.
B) The company pays taxes only to the residence state.
C) The source state mitigates the tax.
D) The company pays taxes to the states with the lowest tax rate.

2

Elsa donated $700 to a home for the aged last year.

In her tax income, which of the following can she declare the donation as?

A) Living expenses
B) Discretionary income
C) Tax deductions
D) Public property

3

Which of the following refers to the seller's guarantee to a consumer of a refund of their purchase price if the product does not perform as expected?

A) Warranty
B) Guarantee
C) Market
D) Strategy

4

Employees put their employers at risk when they show unethical behaviors. These risks may include financial losses.

Which of the following illustrates a company managing its risk concerning its employees' workplace behavior?

A) Encouraging its employees to report misconduct in the workplace.
B) Allowing its employees to utilize their resources for personal use.
C) Permitting its employees to have access to all of its company records.
D) Giving its employees with the capability for changing company policies.

5

Which of the following is the importance of giving the employees enough safety and health information as well as training for businesses?

A) To control the sick leave of employees.
B) To prevent accidents from happening.
C) To ensure higher profits.
D) To increase the morale of employees.

6

Legal procedures are the proceedings in any civil lawsuit or criminal prosecution and, particularly, describe the formal notice or writ used by a court.

Which of the following affects legal procedures?

A) Freedom

B) Jurisdiction

C) Misdemeanor

D) They can protect consumers.

7

From the list of doctrines given below, which of the following prevents a person from insuring a neighbor's house?

A) Doctrine of indemnification

B) Doctrine of insurable interest

C) Doctrine of contribution

D) Doctrine of subrogation

8

Which of the following is a business doing if it monitors laws continuously and performs changes to maintain compliance?

A) Controlling their risks

B) Increasing their liabilities

C) Demonstrating negligence

D) Interpreting contracts

9

What federal organization is responsible for regulating overall workplace safety?

A) Equal Employment Opportunity Commision

B) Occupational Safety and Health Administration

C) Environmental Protection Agency

D) United States Department of Agriculture

10

Ethics are moral principles governing an individual's behavior or the conducting of an activity.

Which of the following statements best describes ethics?

A) Ethics is the concern with moral decision making.

B) Ethics is doing what is in the best interest of the client.

C) Ethics is concerned with human conduct.

D) All of the above.

11

What is the primary responsibility of the Equal Employment Opportunity Commission?

A) Legislating on behalf of pregnant women for constant pay rate during maternity leave.

B) Ensuring the number of men is equal to the number of women in the workplace.

C) Enforcing federal law against discrimination.

D) Enforcing state laws regarding sex, gender, and religion in the workplace.

12

Ms. Bailey was not compelled to pay taxes because she gave a portion of her salary to a charity.

Which of the following explains Ms.Bailey's case?

A) Tax deduction

B) Tax-deferred investment

C) Estate allocation

D) Investment disbursement

13

Which of the following violates the copyright law when someone buys an image-editing software?

A) Copying the software onto a disk for a friend.

B) Selling the software and the software's disk to a third party.

C) Copying the software's disk to make a backup.

D) Creating artwork with the application and selling it.

14

In which of the following tax type do individuals with a high-salary pay a larger percentage of tax?

A) Regressive tax

B) Proportional tax

C) Progressive tax

D) Flat tax

15

Which of the following government regulatory agency is responsible for administering and enforcing antitrust laws to prevent price fixing and unethical competitive practices that include false or misleading advertising?

A) Food and Drug Administration

B) Consumer Product Safety Commission

C) Federal Communications Commission

D) Federal Trade Commission

16

If Amanda receives a $15 tip from her client in addition to $80 as payment for the availed service, what amount does Amanda need to declare to the Internal Revenue Service (IRS) for tax?

A) $15

B) $80

C) $95

D) None, if the payment was in cash.

17

Which of the following are designated or chosen for the decision-making on behalf of the company's owners or shareholders?

A) The industry's professional organization

B) The municipal court system

C) The corporation's board of directors

D) The company's line staff

18

Which of the following issues is the most fundamental principle why ethics needs to be considered?

A) Diversity

B) Safety

C) Respect

D) Privacy

19

Accidents in workplace are costly for both the employees and the employers.

In what aspect does a workplace accident become costly to employees?

A) Lost sales

B) Lost profits

C) Lost production

D) Lost income

20

Sexual harassment is any unwelcome sexual advances or requests for sexual favors, may it be verbal or physical.

When sexual harassment occurs in the workplace, which of the following is it most likely to cause?

A) A hostile work environment
B) Good promotion for the business
C) Urge for employees to work harder
D) Distress to all employees

21

Administrative law is the body of law governing the activities of the government's administrative agencies.

Which of the following is the main responsibility of administrative law?

A) Overturn the decisions of the lower courts.
B) Organize congressional or parliamentary committees.
C) Enforce the regulations of the agency.
D) Explain the constitutional laws.

22

What are the benefits required by the law for the employers to provide their employees?

A) COBRA coverage
B) Medical leave birth for childbirth and worker's compensation
C) Medical insurance plans and retirement plans or pensions
D) Worker's compensation and retirement plans

23

Keywords are entered by internet users in the search field when they access search engines to find information they seek.

Which of the following infringement problems occur if one entity is associated with another person or business without their permission?

A) Auto responders
B) Opt-in e-mail
C) Web endorsements
D) Meta tags

24

Why is it difficult to defend issues regarding ethics?

A) Because identifying what is right or wrong is not always agreed about on.

B) Because the coworkers do not want to report to each other.

C) Because it is not always clear-cut and specific.

D) All of the above.

25

Among the advertising claims listed below, which of the following would the Federal Trade Commission most likely question?

A) "Our diamonds are the finest."

B) "Eat our burgers; they are the best in the world."

C) "Using our cream guarantees no more wrinkles."

D) "Our apple juice gives you more."

26

Businesses need to be aware of the laws which may influence the individuals they do business with as well as the communities where they do their business.

Which of the following is correct about the impact of the law on business?

A) Criminal law only applies to individuals thus it does not govern businesses.

B) Laws, may it be local, international or international, governs businesses.

C) Instead of focusing on legal issues required by national law, business should focus on ethical issues.

D) Corporate laws that are enacted and enforced by the local government should be the priority of businesses.

27

A company received over $600 for its services as payment from another company with which it has a contract agreement.

Which of the following forms should be filed by this company to the Internal Revenue Service (IRS)?

A) Form 1099-Misc

B) Form 1040 EZ

C) Form 1040

D) Form W-9

CONTINUE ▶

28

Which of the following does the government pass to give protection to the property of the business owners?

A) Safety standards
B) Consumer-protection laws
C) Zoning laws
D) Minimum-wage laws

30

An **estate tax** is a tax given on the assets transferred to another individual upon the owner's death.

Which of the following is an example of an estate-tax deduction?

A) Money that is left to friends or distant relatives.
B) Unqualified charitable contributions.
C) Direct transfer of property to the spouse.
D) Valuable art and collectibles left to children.

29

Something of value must be exchanged for a contract to be legally binding. A new businessman signed a lease to rent a small building which he will pay monthly.

Which of the following does rent represent in a legally binding contract?

A) Competent parties
B) Legality
C) Agreement
D) Consideration

31

U.S. Equal Employment Opportunity Commission or EEOC is an agency responsible for enforcing laws against discrimination on a job applicant.

Which of the following is not in the EEOC category for anti-discrimination?

A) Religion
B) National origin
C) Age
D) Actions

Loss-leader pricing refers to a pricing strategy that involves the selling of products near or below its market cost.

Which of the following loss-leader pricing is illegal?

A) Competitors match the price.
B) Customers pay a premium.
C) Products are sold below its cost.
D) Businesses obtain a large profit.

Adverse consequences may be experienced by businesses when they do not follow or comply with the government regulations.

Which of the following are the potential risks for businesses that fail to comply with goverment regulations?

A) Lower stock values, fines, and higher sales
B) Fines, penalties, and bankruptcy
C) Penalties, higher stock values, and lower credibility
D) Bankruptcy, higher sales, and lower stock values

The act or omission that results in harm or injury to others is called a **tort**.

In which of the following situations does a tort occur?

A) A credit card is stolen and used to make several purchases.
B) A pet dog runs into the street and is struck by a vehicle.
C) The renter terminates a one-year lease before it ends.
D) A firework spark ended up on a neighbor's tree causing fire and burning it down.

Which of the following is considered unethical but not illegal for corporate officers?

A) Increasing revenues by booking the demonstration product of the salespersons as goods sold
B) Make a deal with competitors to charge the same prices for some products.
C) Talk with the supplier for a price reduction by proposing future increases in business.
D) Selling stock in the corporation before the announcement of a decline in earnings.

36

Protecting their customers' confidential information is one of the responsibilities of businesses. An employee has leaked classified information about a well-known client that spreads through media resulting in the client and the business to be compromised.

Which of the following should the company do to prevent this kind of unethical behavior?

A) Demand resignation from the employee.

B) Give the clients capabilities to track information.

C) Install an anti-virus software to protect the computer network.

D) Put a password on the computer to restrict access to specific data.

37

Ethics is a system of moral principles. On the other hand, risk management involves identifying, analysis and alleviation of uncertainties regarding investment decisions.

Which of the following associates ethics to the risk management?

A) Risk management is the best form of business ethics.

B) In case of lapses in business ethics, risk management serves as insurance.

C) Adherence to business ethics is the best form of risk management.

D) Risk management is concerned with the ethical treatment of customers.

38

A judge must determine if each party is capable of performing or carrying out an agreement to enforce a contract.

Would a contract be enforceable if a 16-year-old agreed to purchase a car from an adult and then decided that she doesn't want to buy the vehicle?

A) No, in most countries, it is illegal for minors to engage in contracts with adults.

B) No, since an agreement with a minor may be voided by the seller.

C) Yes, if the minor's parent cosigns the contractual agreement for the car purchase.

D) Yes, the breaching of a contract is prevented by the contractual capacity provision.

39

Which of the following is the intention of a business' unethical move in promoting low-priced items that are unavailable for the customers to purchase?

A) Better quality products are offered to the customers.

B) Customers are persuaded to buy more expensive items.

C) The prices advertised by competitors are matched.

D) Sales to the target markets are increased.

Which of the following acts or regulations mandate a publicly traded company to have its code of ethics registered with the Securities and Exchange Commision as well as to ensure that its senior financial officers are aware of the policy?

A) Code of Federal Regulations

B) National Labor Relations Act

C) Sarbanes-Oxley Act

D) Single Audit Act

A **whistle-blower** is an employee that reports the unlawful activities of his/her employers to a government agency or media outlet.

Which of the following is the whistle-blower protected from laws of some local, regional, and national governments?

A) Filing for bankruptcy resulting from poor business investments.

B) Having liens placed on their residential property.

C) Losing their jobs for reporting their employers' wrongdoing.

D) Being held liable for the negligent behavior of minors in their care.

A marketing-research company was hired by a major credit card company to do a survey about the use of consumer credit.

Would it be ethical for the marketing-research company to utilize the information obtained from this survey in a direct marketing campaign?

A) No, research company should not engage in any non-research activities that involve the data collected.

B) No, this information can't be considered as a reliable source of marketing.

C) Yes, the company can use it in any way it wants since they paid for the research.

D) Yes, the consumers know that surveys are a means of obtaining information for advertising.

The act of making products and services available for people to purchase them is called **selling**.

Which of the following situations illustrates an ethical behavior in the sale?

A) Alan increases the prices on its clothing before making a 50%-off sale for the customers to feel right about the amount of money they can save.

B) Sam tells his neighbor she can save $300 by purchasing a vacuum cleaner without the carpet attachment because he has hardwood floors.

C) Mr. Sandler informs Kevin he cannot give him a raise, so he should claim additional expenses on his monthly expense account to compensate for it.

D) Jay tells the customer he can save an additional $55, that instead of the company, he makes his check out to him.

Which of the following situations best illustrates a legal but not ethical concept in business?

A) A group of pharmacists agree to charge the same prices because of the rising costs of prescription medicines.

B) A business goes beyond the letter of the law to preserve the environment for future generations.

C) A top company executive uses questionable accounting practices to manipulate the company's stock price for financial gain.

D) A company imports and sells goods from a company that uses child labor in unsafe conditions in its manufacturing plants.

Which of the following should businesses do to protect their customer data like credit card information?

A) Require all customers to present an ID.
B) Encrypt sensitive records.
C) Accept only cash payments.
D) Use a shared server for storing information.

Ethical businesses attempt to treat their employees equally and not punish those who commit mistakes.

Which of the following illustrates a business manager handling his/her employees unethically?

A) Offering limited part-time options
B) Downsizing the workforce
C) Disciplining a whistle-blower
D) Monitoring use of supplies

Environmental laws are meant for the conservation and protection of the natural environment. Many of these influence the way businesses operate by requiring them to minimize pollution or control waste.

Which of the following is an effect of some environmental laws on businesses?

A) More employees are required.
B) Operating costs are increased.
C) Equipment purchases are limited.
D) Exterior landscapes are controlled.

Companies are required by **full-disclosure laws and regulations** to disclose any information which could influence the value of the firm's stocks.

Which of the following is the importance of full-disclosure laws and regulations?

A) The drop of a stock's par value below its market value is prevented.
B) All information regarding a company's operations is required to be disclosed.
C) Company employees gained the capability to access inside information and use it for personal gain.
D) Give the investors information to allow them in making informed decisions.

49

Business ethics comprises the principles, values, and standards that guide behavior in the world of business.

Which of the following is correct about business ethics?

A) Business ethics is entirely an extension of an individual's own personal ethics.

B) Business ethics is a part of decision making at all levels of work and management.

C) A guide of principles designed to help professionals conduct business honestly and with integrity is called as code of ethics.

D) All of the above

50

Governments develop regulations to assure the safety of the public.

Which of the following facilities are inspected by authorized officials to ensure compliance with safety ordinances?

A) Portable cameras

B) Computer networks

C) Elevators

D) Photocopiers

51

Adam's Company is filing a legal case for financial compensation against Cornell Company for using their trademark illegally.

Which of the following is the first step in this legal case?

A) Request a date to be set for a pretrial conference to clear all the legal issues to be discussed during the trial.

B) Do an examination of discovery for all parties involved in the illegal use of Adams's trademark.

C) Declare a summon that requires the Cornell Company to answer the allegations regarding the misuse of the trademark.

D) File a formal complaint to the court asserting the illegal use of their trademark by the Cornell Company.

52

The Robinson-Patman Act (1936) imposes limits on price discrimination practices wherein customers are charged with different prices for the same product or service.

Which of the following price discrimination is not legal?

A) Prices do not limit competition.

B) Price varies to meet competitor's prices.

C) Prices prevent competition.

D) Buyers have no competition with each other.

The regulation of promotional activities is created generally for advertising content and issues in competition.

Which of the following is the main reason why governments in a free-enterprise economic system regulate and restrict the content of promotional activities?

A) Increase the competition among consumer advocate groups.

B) Protect the consumers from false advertising.

C) Facilitate cooperative advertising programs.

D) Develop additional tax bases.

Can a business partnership exist without a binding agreement and no acknowledgement between each party as partners?

A) No, since income tax documents are filed separately by each party, there will be no proof to show that there is an existing partnership relationship.

B) No, articles of the partnership must be filed by all partnerships so there will a legal record of the relationship in the government.

C) Yes, a relationship may exist under the partnership by implication provision if there is a proof that establishes profit sharing by two or more people.

D) Yes, when three or more people make a specific transaction involving the transfer of responsibilities.

A **contract** is an agreement existing between two or more parties which states that one party will do something in return for something given by the other party.

Which of the following is correct about the legality of contracts?

A) A contract is legally valid only if it is documented in writing and signed by both parties.

B) A judge often makes decisions for cases involving oral contracts between two parties

C) Contingency contracts are not deemed legally binding due to its wide scope.

D) Arbitration is the only way to determine the legality of an implied contract.

In regards to the condition of a product, a manufacturer or a similar party makes and issues a type of guarantee called **warranty**.

Which of the following is correct about warranty?

A) The rules of a warranty are outlined in the UCC.

B) A warranty must be written.

C) A warranty is sometimes legally binding.

D) A warranty is applicable only with products.

CONTINUE ▶

SECTION 3 BUSINESS LAWS & ETHICS

#	Answer	Topic	Subtopic	#	Answer	Topic	Subtopic	#	Answer	Topic	Subtopic	#	Answer	Topic	Subtopic
1	A	TA	S1	15	D	TA	S1	29	D	TA	S1	43	B	TA	S1
2	C	TA	S1	16	C	TA	S1	30	C	TA	S1	44	D	TA	S1
3	A	TA	S1	17	C	TA	S1	31	D	TA	S1	45	A	TA	S1
4	A	TA	S1	18	C	TA	S1	32	C	TA	S1	46	C	TA	S1
5	B	TA	S1	19	D	TA	S1	33	B	TA	S1	47	B	TA	S1
6	B	TA	S1	20	A	TA	S1	34	D	TA	S1	48	D	TA	S1
7	D	TA	S1	21	C	TA	S1	35	C	TA	S1	49	D	TA	S1
8	A	TA	S1	22	B	TA	S1	36	D	TA	S1	50	C	TA	S1
9	B	TA	S1	23	D	TA	S1	37	C	TA	S1	51	D	TA	S1
10	D	TA	S1	24	D	TA	S1	38	C	TA	S1	52	C	TA	S1
11	C	TA	S1	25	D	TA	S1	39	B	TA	S1	53	B	TA	S1
12	A	TA	S1	26	B	TA	S1	40	C	TA	S1	54	C	TA	S1
13	A	TA	S1	27	A	TA	S1	41	C	TA	S1	55	B	TA	S1
14	C	TA	S1	28	C	TA	S1	42	A	TA	S1	56	A	TA	S1

Topics & Subtopics

Code	Description	Code	Description
SA1	Business Laws & Ethics	TA	Business Evironment

CONTINUE ▶

TEST DIRECTION

Read the questions carefully and then choose the ONE best answer to each question.

Be sure to allocate your time carefully so you are able to complete the entire test within the testing session. You may go back and review your answers at any time.

You may use any available space in your test booklet for scratch work.

Questions in this booklet are not actual test questions but they are the samples for commonly asked questions.

This test aims to cover all topics which may appear on the actual test. However some topics may not be covered.

Studying this booklet will be preparing you for the actual test. It will not guarantee improving your test score but it will help you pass your exam on the first attempt.

Some useful tips for answering multiple choice questions;

- Start with the questions that you can easily answer.

- Underline the keywords in the question.

- Be sure to read all the choices given.

- Watch for keywords such as NOT, always, only, all, never, completely.

- Do not forget to answer every question.

1

Lea forgot that she told Sam to update the price list, so instead, he asked Tin to do it.

Which of the following is most likely to happen when there is a lack of coordination among the team members?

A) Accurate calculations

B) High efficiency

C) Effective collaboration

D) Duplicate work

2

A business education teacher aims to develop her student's personal interview skills.

Which of the following would be the most effective instructional resource to use in the lesson?

A) Lectures on how to behave during an interview

B) Presentations about sample interviews

C) Textbooks on how to develop interview skills

D) Videotapes about sample interviews

3

Which of the following acts states business education as a recognized integral part of vocational education?

A) George Barden Act (1946)

B) Smith Hugh Act (1917)

C) George Deen Act (1939)

D) Vocational Education Act (1963)

4

Following every employment interview, an applicant should construct and send the interviewer a follow-up letter.

Which of the following is the primary purpose of a **follow-up letter**?

A) To explain the applicant's qualification.

B) To ask supplemental questions.

C) To submit personal information.

D) To show the applicant's continued interest.

5

Which of the following is the manager's best first step in increasing the energy efficiency of a building built in the 1960s with high heating and cooling costs?

A) Encourage the use of fans and space heaters in the offices.

B) Ask for a list of areas of highest energy loss in the building from the staff.

C) Recommend that the building undergoes a comprehensive energy audit.

D) Replace all incandescent lighting with fluorescent lighting.

In developing a technology plan for schools in a school district, which of the following should be the most fundamental aspect to be considered?

A) Due to digital technologies, the future of learning is less individualized.

B) Compared with average homes, average schools has more internet connectivity.

C) Network capacities are mostly within reach for most schools to meet all their teaching needs.

D) In general, more training is needed for teachers to integrate technology into their lessons.

A college student is working part-time and planning to open a bank account with a $500 initial deposit. He/she is paid twice a week in a paycheck and it is deposited directly into his account.

Which of the following types of accounts should he/she open at the bank?

A) Certificate of deposit
B) Money market
C) Checking
D) Savings

Systematically maintaining files helps in keeping reports, forms, notes, and other documents in a particular location.

Which of the following is less likely encountered by keeping files and documents organized?

A) Misplacing important documents
B) Forgetting important phone numbers
C) Discarding unnecessary paperwork
D) Misusing office equipment

Stress is an organism's response to a situation that causes mental, physical, or emotional feeling of pressure.

Which of the following issue is the main reason why many businesses develop programs and activities that can reduce employee stress?

A) To maintain productivity
B) To eliminate conflict
C) To encourage creativity
D) To exhibit empathy

10

According to the Occupational Safety and Health Act of 1970, which of the following should the employers make their employees aware of?

A) Laws concerning wage and hours of job.

B) Workplace hazards and health issues encountered on the job.

C) Right to have health compensation extending up to a year after job dismissal.

D) The requirements needed for other bonuses and compensation.

11

Understanding oneself helps to understand others.

Which of the following can an individual gain from the sentence given above?

A) Obtaining what you want from others.

B) Helping others to become mature.

C) Doing what others want you to do.

D) Getting along well with others.

12

Which of the following does a person develop when he/she receives a lot of negative feedbacks?

A) Optimism

B) Depression

C) Self-importance

D) Enthusiasm

A **business plan** is a document that presents the basic idea for the business. It is a roadmap for the business that sets goals and plans to achieve those goals.

Which of the following about a business plan is not correct?

A) While developing a business plan, the first step is defining consumer needs that the business will aim to meet.

B) Operations and development part of a business plan offers information on how a product will be produced or a service provided.

C) Offering section of the business plan indicates to an investor how much money is needed.

D) Critical risks are the section of the business plan that gives a clear overall picture of the proposed business.

A **Career Development Plan** is a written list of the short and long-term goals of the employees pertaining to their current and future jobs.

Which of the following about the career development plan is true?

A) It focuses on the employees' needs for growth and development.

B) The purpose of a Career Development Plan is to assist employees in achieving their goals.

C) It helps employees set realistic expectations of career growth by suggesting time frames for certain milestones to happen.

D) All of the above

15

What characteristic describes a person who remains positivite even in tough times during a business venture?

A) Innovation
B) Optimism
C) Organization
D) Determination

16

With which of the following is the process of developing unique ideas associated?

A) Creative thinking
B) Critical thinking
C) Reflective thinking
D) Associative thinking

17

When connecting with others to help them in achieving personal career and professional goals, which of the following is used most?

A) Social networking
B) Educational setting
C) Corporate environment
D) Formal event

18

Career planning is a continuous process of matching career goals and individual capabilities with the opportunities for their fulfillment.

Which of the following about business career plan is not correct?

A) A business career plan includes short-term or long-term SMART goals leading to an ideal career.
B) Assessing personal work-related interests and skills is the first step to develop a business career plan.
C) After you make a career plan, you have to stick to it and do not revise it.
D) It is a dynamic plan which is continuously modified during the career path.

19

Which of the following sets of personal attributes would have the highest positive effect on a person's career advancement and success?

A) Confidence, Energy, Inquisitiveness
B) Confidence Energy Obedience
C) Traditionalism, Confidence, Inquisitiveness
D) Energy, Obedience, Traditionalism

20

Which of the following does a supervisor exhibit when he/she tells an employee about the things he/she can do to improve their job?

A) Constructive criticism
B) Interpersonal relationships
C) Self-control
D) Harassment

21

Which of the following is the most responsible action to take by an individual who commits a mistake?

A) Quit the project.
B) Try to fix it before someone discovers it.
C) Admit committing the mistake.
D) Determine where or who to put the blame.

22

Which of the following practices is the least efficient way for a business leader to build staff morale?

A) Striving to provide resources staff requests.
B) Recognizing staff publicly for their exemplary performance.
C) Relieving staff of the pressure of making leadership decisions.
D) Involving staff in planning and evaluating business activities

23

Which of the following is a benefit of maintaining a sense of humor to be a good team member?

A) It helps in easing any tension that arises.
B) It gives more self-confidence.
C) It keeps emotions under control.
D) It improves skills in decision-making.

24

Goals are set to help a business grow and accomplish its objectives.

Which of the following is correct about company goals?

A) Goals are essential only for new companies.

B) All company goals are vague.

C) All goals are the same at every company.

D) Goals cannot be accomplished without the company employees' dedication.

25

Critical thinking is a clear, rational, open-minded and disciplined thinking informed by evidence.

Critical reasoning is the process of using critical thinking, knowledge & experience to find solutions to the problems.

Which of the following is/are the integral parts of critical thinking process?

A) A good foundation of knowledge

B) Willingness to ask questions

C) Ability to recognize new answers

D) All of the above

26

What action should a business leader take to create collaborative relationships among staff?

A) Encourage out-of-work get-togethers.

B) Group employees based on performance and skill.

C) Promote respect and effective communication.

D) Encourage staff to resolve problems on their own.

27

Which of the following method is shown by employees who are doing research and preparing reports to recommend a change?

A) Persuasion

B) Management

C) Leadership

D) Enthusiasm

28

Anastasia is offered a new high-paying job but it will require her to move from a rural to an urban area of Michigan.

Which of the following is the most crucial point for her to consider in decision-making?

A) If her new salary will be in a higher tax bracket.

B) If the costs of living will offset her higher salary.

C) If a change in job would have an effect on her credit rating.

D) If her current 401(k) retirement plan can be rolled over.

29

The person responsible for the planning and execution of a project is usually the same.

Who among the following is typically assigned in project planning?

A) Project manager

B) Project assistant

C) Project scheduler

D) Project coordinator

30

Which of the following is not a primary responsibility of the Occupational Safety and Health Administration?

A) Driving commercial diving requirements

B) Regulating work walking

C) Establishing requirements for electrical standards

D) Monitoring the development of X-ray equipment

31

A **strategy** refers to a plan of action or policy designed to achieve a major or overall aim.

Which of the following strategies would enable teachers to work effectively with students from diverse backgrounds?

A) Differentiated instruction

B) Teacher-centered instruction

C) Lecture-centered instruction

D) Demonstration-centered instruction

32

Which of the following would be the first step to take for a student planning to pursue a career in business?

A) Determine the educational requirements for different positions.

B) Make a resume that includes relevant courses and experience.

C) Identify the career paths having the highest growth potential.

D) Complete an aptitude and personal interests assessment.

33

National Business Education Association (NBAE) is a private and largest professional organization of its kind in the United States.

Which of the following statements is one of the objectives of NBAE?

A) To promote students with terminal degrees.

B) To promote legislation in place of its members.

C) To promote professional development in all United States Department of Labor clusters.

D) To manage the teacher evaluation process.

34

In an organization, its **mission statement** is a very personal and deliberate declaration representing its legitimacy to the world and shows its desired public image.

Which of the following is the importance of writing a mission statement?

A) It will show the company's achievements.

B) It will help clarify the philosophies of the company.

C) It will show relations that can be made within the company.

D) It will give employees their sales goals.

35

Which of the following can be controlled by employees that sets realistic goals and standards for themselves instead of wanting perfection everytime?

A) Group participation

B) Work schedule

C) Ability to advance

D) Level of stress

36

Continuous improvement involves an on-going effort to make improvements either on a process, a product or a service.

Which of the following illustrates a continuous improvement?

A) Reducing the defect levels to 2.8 per million units manufactured.

B) Doing a yearly self-assessment and improvement process.

C) Providing the managers a full responsibility for product quality.

D) Choosing the best supplier possible.

37

Team organizational design involves groups of individuals formed from different functional areas for problem-solving and exploration of possibilities.

Which of the following is the importance of utilizing a team organizational structure?

A) It increases competency among employees.

B) It gives each department the complete autonomy to create a more innovative approach.

C) It removes functional barriers among the departments for the working relationships to strengthen and improve efficiency.

D) It creates a central department which will facilitate the decision-making process.

38

Which of the following is the difference between a goal and vision?

A) A goal is precise and measurable.

B) A goal is abstract and vague.

C) A goal can have different meanings to different people.

D) A goal and a vision has no difference and are the same.

39

As proposed by Abraham Maslow's **hierarchy of needs**, motivation results from a person's attempt at fulfilling the five basic needs which can create internal pressures that can affect a person's behavior.

Which of the following needs can a manager fulfill if he makes sure each of the employees knows one another, encourages cooperative teamwork, be an accessible and kind supervisor and promotes an excellent work-life balance?

A) Esteem needs

B) Social needs

C) Self-actualization needs

D) Physiological needs

40

Organizational design is a process that involves managers assessing the tasks, functions, and goals of the business.

Which of the following organizational design types are sales and marketing, finance and accounting, customer service, and human resource classified into?

A) Simple
B) Matrix
C) Network
D) Functional

41

What action should a business leader take to promote the staff's professional development?

A) Encouraging staff to participate in development programs.
B) Requiring staff to attend development programs.
C) Giving demerits to staff who fail to participate in development programs.
D) Making professional development criteria for evaluation of staff.

42

Chain of command involves a centralized organization directing its authority from the top management towards the lower one through hierarchal channels, involving only a few top managers in-charge of overall decision making.

Which of the following is the biggest disadvantage of centralized authority in the chain of command hierarchy?

A) It results in a very slow decision-making process.
B) Less work will be disseminated.
C) The employees' duties cannot be tracked.
D) In the lower levels of the chain of command, employees are less efficient.

43

SWOT analysis is a decision-making process also known as situational analysis. The primary purpose of the situational analysis is for marketers to understand the current and potential environments.

Which of the following is the importance of evaluating managerial decisions using a SWOT Analysis for a company?

A) It analyzes obligations, weak points, opportunities, and threats.
B) It analyzes strengths, weaknesses, opportunities, and time.
C) It analyzes strengths, weaknesses, opportunities, and threats.
D) It analyzes time, weaknesses, obligations, and threats.

Leadership is the act of leading people in an organization towards the achievement of goals by influencing employee behaviors in several ways.

In which of the following a leader would best motivate his employees?

A) Giving bonuses and longer work off as a reward.

B) Determining employees' needs and wants and appreciating their hard work.

C) Giving detailed work for them to make fewer mistakes.

D) Continually emphasizing the mission of the company and the employees' role in making the business successful.

In an organization, the role of a leader can be assigned formally by his or her position, like the manager or department head, and can also be assumed informally by an employee possessing a certain charisma which attracts others to follow.

Which of the following is the difference between unassigned and assigned leadership roles?

A) Motivating employees is more critical in assigned leadership roles.

B) Personality traits are more critical in unassigned leadership roles.

C) Organizing and directing people to perform tasks is more critical in unassigned leadership roles.

D) Charismatic influence is more critical in assigned leadership roles.

The term of "**Collective barganing**" has its roots in the 18th century. It was first used in 1891 by **Beatrice Webb**, a founder of the field of industrial relations in Britain.

Which of the following explains collective bargaining?

A) Negotiating workers' salaries, benefits, and working conditions with the administration and the workers' association.

B) Implementing new plans from the head department to each personnel.

C) Ensuring that any legal proceeding is based on established judicial rules, practices, and safeguards.

D) All of the above.

The **Distributive Education Clubs of America (DECA)** is an international association composed of high school and college students, teachers of marketing, management, and entrepreneurship in business, finance, hospitality, as well as marketing sales and service.

Which of the following will best prepare the students in learning how to effectively operate a school store through an assisted company by DECA sponsor?

A) Researching management styles

B) Designing store logos

C) Participating in team-building games

D) Taking part in on-the-job coaching

Teachers use **instructional strategies** which are techniques that help students become independent, strategic learners.

Which of the following instructional strategies illustrates a common business practice that engages students?

A) Role-playing
B) Simulation
C) Journal writing
D) Brainstorming

Job shadowing is a type job training in which a student can become familiar with a different job. During this training students spend a day with a competent and they can follow and observe a trained and experienced employee.

Which of the following is the best reason for beginning a job-shadowing program for high school students?

A) To build a good rapport with those in the community.
B) To show students good work ethics and communication skills.
C) To assess students' aptitudes and skill levels in the workplace.
D) To provide students with working experience in a career interest.

The **two-factor theory**, developed by Herzberg, is a theory of workplace motivation based on the assumption that there are two sets of factors influencing motivation in a workplace.

The presence of **motivators** cause employees to work harder, and absence of **hygiene factors** such as work conditions and company policies cause them to become unmotivated.

Which of the following can eliminate employee dissatisfaction according to Herzberg?

A) Discovering the correct balance between hygiene factors and motivators.
B) Remedying the causes of dissatisfaction.
C) Giving another task to be done.
D) Lessening workload of each employee.

Assessment methods involve strategies, techniques, tools, and instruments for collecting information to determine the extent to which students display desired learning outcomes.

Which of the following assessment methods is needed by a teacher who wants to evaluate student progress using a performance-based approach?

A) Multiple-choice questions
B) Open-ended questions
C) Matching questions
D) True-false questions

Performance-based assessment assesses a students' ability to apply the skills and knowledge learned from a unit or units of study.

When designing a unit on sponsorship, using which of the following as a performance-based assessment is the most appropriate for a sports-marketing teacher in assessing student learning of the objective?

A) The students' work for a local sports team in getting sponsors and contracts.
B) The students' research about the sponsorship contracts of a major sports franchise.
C) The students' evaluation report about current school sports sponsors by comparing and contrasting them.
D) The students' research paper regarding how sponsorships benefit sports.

SECTION 4 CAREER & BUSINESS EDUCATION

#	Answer	Topic	Subtopic	#	Answer	Topic	Subtopic	#	Answer	Topic	Subtopic	#	Answer	Topic	Subtopic
1	D	TA	S4	14	B	TA	S4	27	A	TA	S4	40	D	TA	S4
2	D	TA	S5	15	B	TA	S4	28	B	TA	S4	41	D	TA	S4
3	D	TA	S5	16	A	TA	S4	29	A	TA	S4	42	A	TA	S4
4	D	TA	S4	17	A	TA	S4	30	D	TA	S4	43	C	TA	S4
5	C	TA	S4	18	C	TA	S4	31	A	TA	S5	44	B	TA	S4
6	D	TA	S5	19	A	TA	S4	32	D	TA	S5	45	B	TA	S4
7	C	TA	S5	20	A	TA	S4	33	B	TA	S5	46	A	TA	S4
8	A	TA	S4	21	C	TA	S4	34	B	TA	S4	47	A	TA	S5
9	A	TA	S4	22	C	TA	S4	35	D	TA	S4	48	D	TA	S5
10	B	TA	S4	23	A	TA	S4	36	B	TA	S4	49	D	TA	S5
11	D	TA	S4	24	D	TA	S4	37	C	TA	S4	50	A	TA	S4
12	B	TA	S4	25	D	TA	S4	38	A	TA	S4	51	B	TA	S5
13	D	TA	S4	26	C	TA	S4	39	B	TA	S4	52	A	TA	S5

Topics & Subtopics

Code	Description	Code	Description
SA4	Career Development	TA	Business Evironment
SA5	Business Education		

Unauthorized copying any part of this page is illegal.
66
CONTINUE ▶

TEST DIRECTION

DIRECTIONS

Read the questions carefully and then choose the ONE best answer to each question.

Be sure to allocate your time carefully so you are able to complete the entire test within the testing session. You may go back and review your answers at any time.

You may use any available space in your test booklet for scratch work.

Questions in this booklet are not actual test questions but they are the samples for commonly asked questions.

This test aims to cover all topics which may appear on the actual test. However some topics may not be covered.

Studying this booklet will be preparing you for the actual test. It will not guarantee improving your test score but it will help you pass your exam on the first attempt.

Some useful tips for answering multiple choice questions;

- Start with the questions that you can easily answer.

- Underline the keywords in the question.

- Be sure to read all the choices given.

- Watch for keywords such as NOT, always, only, all, never, completely.

- Do not forget to answer every question.

1

Internet is a means of connecting computers that are anywhere in the world with the use of routers and servers.

Which of the following is the benefit that businesses receive by using the Internet?

A) The ability to call employees on the road.
B) Faster connections with suppliers
C) Improved methods of manufacturing.
D) More comfortable use of satellite radio.

2

A group of friends is working on a project together, but they are far away from each other geographically.

Which of the following software would enable them to share files and work on documents together easily?

A) Spyware
B) Shareware
C) Groupware
D) Freeware

3

A **digital signature**, which is also known as an electronic signature, guarantees the authenticity of an electronic document in digital communication.

In digital signatures, which of the following security measures (encryption techniques) are used to provide proof of original documentation?

A) Proxy
B) Token
C) Biometrics
D) Authentication

4

Why is using a network switch more preferable than using a network hub?

A) Because a network switch reduces the network traffic.
B) Because a network switch connects a computer directly to the internet.
C) Because a network switch prevents all viruses from spreading.
D) Because a network switch strengthens password security.

CONTINUE ▶

5

Which of the following should help find information on the Internet specifically about business licenses when all other searches focus on drivers' licenses?

A) + business + license - driver

B) "business license" driver

C) BUSINESS LICENSE

D) + business + license

6

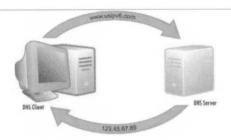

The internet's system for the conversion of alphabetic names into numeric addresses is the **Domain Name System** (DNS).

What is the role of a DNS?

A) It converts a domain name into a binary.

B) It translates a domain name into a hex.

C) It translates a domain name into an IP.

D) It changes a domain name into a URL.

7

The internal network of computers within an organization is called an **intranet**.

Intranet capabilities allow employees to share the business's information with which of the following?

A) Each other

B) Former employees

C) Competitors

D) Customers

8

The computer's operating system is composed of components necessary to run all of the computer applications and programs.

Which of the following is a computer capable of if its operating system that allows the user to open and use more than one software program simultaneously?

A) Multithreading

B) Multitasking

C) Multiprocessing

D) Multi-user

69

CONTINUE ▶

9

What kind of disaster planning is being implemented if copies of records are stored in a building far away from the main building of the company?

A) Establishing a system for record keeping.
B) Computerizing valuable business information.
C) Keeping potential lawsuits in mind.
D) Storing information off-site.

10

Which of the following file extensions should be checked when scanning for viruses in a drive?

A) .wav (Audio File Format)
B) .exe (Executable File Format)
C) .pdf (Portable Document Format)
D) .jpg (Joint Photographic Experts Format)

11

The **digital footprint** is all the stuff left behind as an individual use the Internet or on digital devices.

Which of the following best describes what a digital footprint is?

A) An online digital identity.
B) It is a technological interaction which can be traced back to an individual.
C) An image embedded in a word processing document.
D) An erasable online interaction.

12

Which of the following computer applications aids in the identification and removal of duplicate records, incomplete data fields, and expired data, as well as keeping a database of relevant data that facilitates in good decision making?

A) Data cleansing
B) Environmental scanning
C) Electronic data interchange
D) Tabulation analysis

13

Which of the following is not a correct definition?

A) Internet addressing is developed in 1984 and named as Domain Name System (DNS)

B) A web address is also known as Uniform Resource Locator (URL)

C) The protocol for transferring web files is known as Hypertext Transfer Protocol (HTTP)

D) Hypertext Markup Language (HTML) is an operating system that transfer data to and from a hard drive.

14

"Manila is the capital of the Philippines"

What type of information does the statement given above give?

A) Criticism

B) Factual

C) Unproven

D) Opinion

15

Which of the following refers to a graphical representation of two variables that are used in determining cause and effect?

A) Scatter diagram

B) Histogram

C) Flow chart

D) Check sheet

16

The standard used to define a method of exchanging data over a computer network is called a **protocol**.

Which of the protocols given below is used for sending email?

A) HTTP

B) TCP/IP

C) SMTP

D) FTP

17

How can an image be successfully converted from BMP to JPEG format?

A) By changing the image file extension

B) By compressing the file

C) By using the "Save As" command

D) By renaming the image

CONTINUE ▶

18

Employing graphs and charts in conveying and summarizing information is an effective form of presenting results and relationships. One type of charts typically used is the **pie chart**.

Which of the following can a pie chart be effectively used for?

A) For communicating changing values or percentages in relation with each other but is not related with time.

B) For comparison of qualities of two variables to clearly show changes over time.

C) For providing a visual representation of large variations over space.

D) For identification of the parts of a subject and their spatial or functional relationship.

19

A **file format** is a structure of how information is stored in a computer file.

Which file format would be the most appropriate when data from a spreadsheet needs to be imported into a database package?

A) CSV (Comma Separated Values)

B) RTF (Rich Text Format)

C) HTML (Hypertext Markup Language)

D) PDF (Portable Document Format)

20

An **operating system** is the most important software that runs on a computer. It manages the computer's memory and processes, as well as all of its software and hardware.

Which of the following is NOT a function of the Operating System?

A) Memory management

B) Database management

C) Process management

D) Disk management

21

The contract existing between the licensor and purchaser that establishes the purchaser's right to use the software is called an **end-user license agreement (EULA)** or **software license agreement**.

Which of the following would show a violation of the EULA?

A) Jena lends her laptop to Mike for him to use the programs installed on her computer.

B) Lea downloaded demo software from a company's website and shared it with her friends.

C) Kevin gave his students copies of a single-license program purchased by the school.

D) To make a software program more functional for her needs, Lisa, a computer programmer enhances it.

22

In cases of fire or power outages, which of the following can a financial business do to reduce the risk of losing its computer data?

A) Monitor the data-transmission rates.

B) Perform backup procedures.

C) Use of encryption techniques.

D) Implementing an authorization process.

23

A professor is discussing with his students the importance of **firewalls**.

What would the professor tell his class about the primary function of firewalls?

A) Restrict how data exits the system.

B) Replace host security problems.

C) Provide complete confidentiality.

D) Check all incoming data for viruses.

CONTINUE ▶

The information delievered immediately after its collection is called **real-time data (RTD)**.

In which of the following situations would RTD be most useful?

A) An e-commerce firm prepares an order to ship materials to its custimers from their warehouse.

B) An accounting firm prepares taxes for numerous corporations quarterly.

C) A marketing firm conducting a statistical analysis of the results from the customer satisfaction survey.

D) A brokerage firm wants to enable their clients to access and see their investments' current status.

Identity-Based Encryption (IBE) is an essential primitive ID-based cryptography.

Which of the following reasons is IBE preferred than the other forms of encryption, in the field of business?

A) It has a superior key-management and key-recovery infrastructure.

B) It ensures message security by using digital certificates.

C) It requires servers to store and locate the encryption keys.

D) Upon demand, it automatically generates a public key.

A software monitors data in real time, compares data to a standard, as well as instructs the system to make adjustments if a data is outside tolerances.

Which of the following would this type of software be most useful?

A) Gathering information regarding the buying patterns of individual customers.

B) Obtaining new products when inventory reaches a certain level.

C) Comparing the average shelf life of the same product from different brands.

D) Balancing the sales recorded with the cash received.

Which of the following is being protected when using security software to lessen the risk of unauthorized access on confidential data?

A) Intranet systems

B) Spam email

C) Corporate policies

D) Intercom systems

28

Fraudulence is the act of committing an intentionally false act meant to cause harm or deceive.

Which of the following describes a fraudulent e-mail that seeks to verify personal information?

A) Crowdsourcing

B) Data mining

C) Phishing

D) Spam

29

Worm software mostly relies on security failures on the target computer to access it.

Which of the following best describes the malicious nature of worm software?

A) Sending data from a host computer to another unauthorized entity.

B) Deleting or altering essential files stored on an infected computer.

C) Self-replicating to spread across networks to other computers.

D) Giving a remote hacker unauthorized access to a network computer.

30

Name and address book (NAB) is a book or a database used for storing entries called contacts.

Which of the following is the purpose of a name and address book in an email package?

A) Keeping the list of previously visited URL's.

B) Keeping a list of all contacts and their email addresses.

C) Attaching a file like a word document to a message.

D) Attaching an email signature to an email.

31

• It is associated with the processing of comparison speed.

• It is a method of measuring the raw speed of a computer's processor.

• Its measurement doesn't take into account other factors such as the computer's I/O speed or processor architecture.

Which of the following is explained above?

A) CPS (Characters Per Second)

B) FFT (Fast Fourier Transform)

C) MIPS (Million Instructions Per Second)

D) MPG (Moving Picture Experts Group)

32

A **MAC address** identifies each device on a network and is manufactured into every network card and cannot be changed.

Which of the following defines MAC?

A) Memory Address Corruption
B) Media Access Code
C) Mediocre Apple Computer
D) Media Access Control

33

SSL is the standard security technology for establishing an encrypted link between a web server and a browser. This link ensures that all data passed between the web server and browsers remain private and integral.

What does SSL stand for?

A) Secure system login
B) System socket layer
C) Secure socket layer
D) Secure system login

34

Operations involve the day-to-day activities needed for a business to function continuously.

Which of the following controls the costs and increases the productivity to sustain the operations function?

A) Supply of money
B) Hiring of employees
C) Use of technology
D) Type of management

35

There are some rules and conventions for communication between network devices. Networking computers use connecting devices and set up of strict regulations for communication to take place.

Which of the options refers to the rules and regulations of computer communication?

A) Internet
B) Protocols
C) Browser
D) Web

PPTP is an obsolete method for implementing virtual private networks, with many known security issues.

What does PPTP stand for?

A) Point to Point Transfer Protocol

B) Point to Point Traffic Protocol

C) Point to Point Tunneling Protocol

D) Point to Point Transmission Protocol

One of the essential parts of a computer system is the **motherboard**. A motherboard houses many of the computer's crucial components including the central processing unit (CPU), memory and connectors for input and output devices.

Which of the following would indicate that the motherboard battery has failed?

A) Files on the hard disk are lost and corrupted.

B) Operating system passwords are lost.

C) The hardware settings, as well as the virtual memory, are reverted back to default values.

D) The hardware settings, as well as the current date and time, are reverted back to default values.

38

Mining means extracting something useful or valuable from a base substance, such as mining gold from the earth.

Web log data mining is the gathering of information over the World Wide Web.

In business environment, weblog data mining can be used for which of the following?

A) To understand customer behavior
B) To evaluate the effectiveness of a particular web site
C) To help quantify the success of a marketing campaign
D) All of the above

39

Technology Application is the application of technology tools and devices in the teaching and learning processes.

Which of the following technology applications is best to use for forecasting and performing calculations?

A) Presentation
B) Database
C) Word processor
D) Spreadsheet

40

Data mining involves the automated analysis of large data sets for identification of patterns. There are two types of data mining, the parallel and the distributed mining.

Which of the following is the advantage of parallel data mining over the distributed data mining?

A) In parallel data mining, the knowledge differs between data sets and the global unit.
B) Parallel data mining relies on data partitioning and global blending.
C) In parallel data mining, an algorithm is applied to the entire data set.
D) Communication occurs among multiple process units in parallel data mining.

SECTION 5 INFORMATION TECHNOLOGY

#	Answer	Topic	Subtopic	#	Answer	Topic	Subtopic	#	Answer	Topic	Subtopic	#	Answer	Topic	Subtopic
1	B	TA	S3	11	B	TA	S3	21	C	TA	S3	31	C	TA	S3
2	C	TA	S3	12	A	TA	S3	22	B	TA	S3	32	D	TA	S3
3	D	TA	S3	13	D	TA	S3	23	A	TA	S3	33	C	TA	S3
4	A	TA	S3	14	B	TA	S3	24	D	TA	S3	34	C	TA	S3
5	A	TA	S3	15	A	TA	S3	25	B	TA	S3	35	B	TA	S3
6	C	TA	S3	16	C	TA	S3	26	D	TA	S3	36	C	TA	S3
7	A	TA	S3	17	C	TA	S3	27	A	TA	S3	37	D	TA	S3
8	B	TA	S3	18	A	TA	S3	28	C	TA	S3	38	D	TA	S3
9	D	TA	S3	19	A	TA	S3	29	C	TA	S3	39	D	TA	S3
10	B	TA	S3	20	B	TA	S3	30	B	TA	S3	40	C	TA	S3

Topics & Subtopics

Code	Description	Code	Description
SA3	Information Technology	TA	Business Evironment

CONTINUE ▶

TEST DIRECTION

DIRECTIONS

Read the questions carefully and then choose the ONE best answer to each question.

Be sure to allocate your time carefully so you are able to complete the entire test within the testing session. You may go back and review your answers at any time.

You may use any available space in your test booklet for scratch work.

Questions in this booklet are not actual test questions but they are the samples for commonly asked questions.

This test aims to cover all topics which may appear on the actual test. However some topics may not be covered.

Studying this booklet will be preparing you for the actual test. It will not guarantee improving your test score but it will help you pass your exam on the first attempt.

Some useful tips for answering multiple choice questions;

- Start with the questions that you can easily answer.

- Underline the keywords in the question.

- Be sure to read all the choices given.

- Watch for keywords such as NOT, always, only, all, never, completely.

- Do not forget to answer every question.

CONTINUE ▶

1

The legal agreement wherein a bank or other creditor lends money in exchange for the debtor's property title is called a **mortgage**.

On the other hand, a **government bond** is a bond that a national government issue typically with a guarantee of paying the periodic interest payments and repay the face value on the date of maturity.

Which of the following do mortgages and government bonds belong to?

A) Unrated investments

B) Debt instruments

C) Interest-free services

D) Equity products

2

Which of the following certification is required by an individual to be capable of evaluating companies and industries, and do buy, sell, as well as hold recommendations for certain securities?

A) Certified Financial Planner (CFP)

B) Chartered Financial Analyst (CFA)

C) Certified Stock Broker (CSB)

D) Chartered Financial Consultant (ChFC)

3

PPBS is a budgeting system developed in the 1940's which is used to develop the cost of programs.

What does PPBS stand for?

A) Planning Projects Budgeting Service

B) Projects and Programs Budgeting Service

C) Program Projected Budgeting System

D) Planning, Programming, Budgeting System

4

Companies keep financial records containing the lists of transactions made within the business.

Which of the following type of financial records is necessary in order to keep track of the business' transactions?

A) Operating procedure

B) Accounts receivable

C) Tax identification

D) Payroll information

CONTINUE ▶

5

A **business record** is a document that contains business dealings.

Which of the following type of business records can a firm use to track its customers' buying habits and discover which products are popular and which are not?

A) Marketing budget

B) Annual report

C) Forecast

D) Invoice

6

Which of the following market structures do companies show mutual interdependence?

A) Oligopoly

B) Competitive markets

C) Monopoly

D) Monopsony

7

The market wherein debt instruments are traded is known as the **debt market**. Debt instruments are assets demanding fixed payments to be paid to the holder typically with an interest rate.

Which of the following do debt markets and equity markets buy and sell, respectively?

A) Grain, Gold

B) Gold, Government bonds

C) Government bonds, Corporate stock

D) Corporate stock, Certificates of deposit

8

Internal risks are the risks that stem from the organization.

Which of the following is an example of a business controlling its internal risks?

A) A service business hires illegal immigrants and gives them low wages.

B) A law firm lets its malpractice insurance to lapse.

C) A retailer sells a good at a lower price.

D) A manufacturer regularly inspects and maintains its equipments.

9

Businesses analyze financial information as a guide in their decision making.

What decision should a business make when it shows that a small business's customer base, as well as its profitability, have grown steadily over the past five months?

A) Hiring an additional salesperson
B) Monitoring trends in the industry
C) Liquidating of major assets
D) Getting a loan for equipment repairs

10

An **income statement** reports the financial performance of a company over a certain accounting period.

Which of the following is shown in the income statement of a company over a period of time?

A) The company's equity
B) The company's profitability
C) The company's liabilities
D) The company's reliability

11

Which of the following correctly describes today's purchasing function?

A) The focus of purchasing today shifted from a relational to a transactional one.
B) Purchasing is developing into strategic supply management.
C) A broad supplier base is desired because purchasing prices are lowered.
D) Supplier opportunism typically results from relationships with the suppliers.

12

Which of the following shows the basic calculation used in analyzing an income statement providing an exact picture of a company's financial performance?

A) Sales plus operating costs
B) Income minus expenses
C) Revenue plus sales
D) Assets minus liabilities

13

The **interest rate**, expressed as the percent of the principal amount, is the amount that a lender charges to a borrower for their use of the lender's asset.

Which of the following is the effect of falling interest rates?

A) The stock prices decrease.

B) The stock prices increase.

C) No effect on stock prices.

D) The decline of the stock market.

14

The work interruption caused by majority of the employees refusal to work is called a **labor strike**.

What kind of risk is a labor strike against a major employer?

A) Internal

B) Human

C) Natural

D) Economic

15

A **merger** is a deal that combines two existing companies into one new company.

In the finance industry, how is the merger called when Love Cash Bank has merged with Built to Last Insurance Company?

A) Licensing

B) Tactical planning

C) Convergence

D) Consolidation

16

When giving product information to clients, finance professionals should keep the clients' point-of-view in mind.

Which of the following should finance professionals use regarding this?

A) Simple explanations

B) Financial acronyms

C) Standard responses

D) Technical terms

17

Financial statements consist of reports regarding the financial result and condition, as well as cash flows of an organization.

Which of the following is not a standard financial statement?

A) Shareholder sheet

B) Cash flow statement

C) Balance sheet

D) Income statement

18

Which of the following situations illustrates a less impact on employment when the effective minimum wage is increased?

A) The demand for labor is decreasing.

B) The demand for labor is unit elastic.

C) The demand for labor is a derived demand.

D) The demand for labor is relatively inelastic.

19

A **virtual auditor** employs various reasoning processes on reviewing financial transactions and processes continuously to determine violations in compliance and errors.

Which of the following is used to identify very similar, but not exactly alike, financial system transactions?

A) Contextual reasoning

B) Cross-source reasoning

C) Comparative reasoning

D) Temporal reasoning

20

A **loan application** is a document showing the borrower's income, debt, and other expenses in order to identify their credit worthiness and some necessary information on the target property.

Which of the following should a bank review about the applicant before approving a loan application?

A) Brand preferences

B) Inflation rate

C) Performance goals

D) Debt ratio

21

Environmental scanning involves collecting and interpretation of relevant data in an environment such as an office which can be used in planning or development.

Which of the following makes environmental scanning important?

A) Potential threats
B) New products
C) Foreign markets
D) Competitors' internal environments

22

Businesses need to record different financial information for a specified duration of time.

Which of the following technological tools do businesses use for archiving financial records?

A) Web-development programs
B) Online cloud storage
C) Direct-response software
D) Electronic data interchange

23

Employees are hired to perform specific jobs within the company.

Which of the following is involved when orienting new employees?

A) Reviewing their previous education
B) Developing a compensation package
C) Scheduling a periodic review
D) Giving a specialized training

24

A consumer's income and background may influence her decisions on her purchases.

Which of the following does a utility reveal about a consumer?

A) Income
B) Preferences
C) Influences
D) Background

25

When does a more equal distribution of income occur?

A) When the national sales tax is more regressive.
B) When the income taxes are more progressive.
C) When the unemployment rate becomes higher.
D) When the business owners earn more profits.

26

The central banking system of the United States is the Federal Reserve System.

Which of the following is not part of Federal Reserve System's primary policy?

A) Setting reserve requirements
B) Changing the discount rate
C) Conducting open-market operations
D) Borrowing from foreign governments

27

After a customer withdraws money from an **Automated Teller Machine (ATM)**, which of the following would likely happen?

A) The server's connection is established.

B) The system verifies that the customer has an account.

C) The debt is posted to the account.

D) The customer's access privileges are checked.

28

A theoretical perspective argues that voter behavior is heavily influenced by the economic conditions in their country at the time of the election. It combines the disciplines of political science and economics using econometric techniques.

Based on the information given above, which of the following is the basis for consumers to buy or not to buy some goods and services?

A) Economic votes

B) Limited wants

C) Capital investment

D) Gross income

29

In relation to a business's financial information, which of the following shows an unethical behavior of a businessperson?

A) In order to develop a budget, a manager reviewed the financial records of the business.

B) An auditor verifies if the financial statement of a corporation is accurate.

C) An unauthorized employee examines the financial information of a client.

D) To be able to process a loan, a banker requests for the business' financial information.

30

A lending investment involves a lender allowing a borrower to lend his/her money during a time period with a specified fee or interest rate.

Which of the following is an example of a lending investment?

A) Bonds

B) Antiques

C) Homes

D) Stocks

31

Valuation involves the process wherein the current worth of an asset, or a company is determined.

Which of the following valuations determines the straight-line decrease in value of an asset?

A) Enterprise value

B) Replacement value

C) Salvage value

D) Market value

32

Financial information management involves collecting, maintaining, and storing of financial data.

Which of the following is a primary responsibility of financial information management?

A) Negotiating contracts with vendors

B) Reporting of financial transactions

C) Implementing policies on sales

D) Development of new products

33

A company found that the average cost of production of 5 units of their product is $100, while it is $150 for the production of 6 units of the same product.

What would be the marginal cost of increasing the output from 5 to 6 units of the product?

A) $75

B) $100

C) $150

D) $400

34

A **stock market table** shows the traders the history and the current performance of stocks in the market.

What do the numbers in a stock table's 52-week high and low column show a trader?

A) If there is an overvalue in the stock price.

B) The price range of stocks within the year.

C) The range where the stock price should be present.

D) The best prices for the stock.

CONTINUE ▶

35

Public corporations are required by the government to have an independent author to assure that accurate information is given by the corporation to its stockholders and potential investors.

Which of the following are verified by an independent auditor in a public corporation?

A) Accounting philosophies

B) Diversification efforts

C) Selling policies

D) Financial reports

36

For finance professionals to be able to perform their jobs, they need to acquire certification or licensure, as required by many jurisdictions.

Which of the following certification is needed to aid clients in reducing their debt, growing their wealth, as well as saving for their retirement?

A) Certified Financial Planner (CFP)

B) Chartered Market Technician (CMT)

C) Certified Tax Specialist (CTS)

D) Certified Loan Officer (CLO)

37

Financial information is a record consisting of the financial activities and position of a business, person, or other entity.

Which of the following factors is also needed for financial information to be reliable?

A) Biased

B) Relevant

C) Complete

D) Understandable

38

Which of the following is a financial report containing estimations of when, where, and how much money will move into and out of the business in a given timeframe to determine if loan applicants have enough money to operate?

A) Petty-cash summary

B) Payment voucher

C) Cash-flow statement

D) Corporation charter

CONTINUE ▶

39

A **public good** is a good wherein individuals cannot exclude from use, and the amount of its consumption does not reduce its availability to others.

Which is an example of a public good?

A) National defense

B) Health insurance payments

C) Water supply from a public utility

D) Availability of imported products in the market

40

A financial institution is an establishment responsible for conducting financial transactions like loans, deposits, and investments.

Which of the following describes financial institutions that follow government regulations?

A) Being ethical

B) In mediation

C) Being independent

D) In compliance

41

A **credit plan** is a plan allocating credits to commercial property policyholders with multiple locations.

Which of the following refers to a credit plan that demands for a contract to be signed, a down payment, as well as a balance to be paid over a specific period?

A) Revolving

B) Regular

C) Open

D) Installment

42

Which of the following are the softwares or the printables that help in planning and managing a business's income and expenses?

A) Organizational charts

B) Statistical information

C) Legal data

D) Budgeting tools

Which of the following accounting system reports financial information that aids businesses to determine if they have the necessary budget for hiring additional employees as well as if there is a need for the cost reduction?

A) Financial

B) Computerized

C) Manual

D) Management

Which of the following is represented in the concavity of a production possibilities curve?

A) A decreasing opportunity cost

B) A constant returns to scale

C) The law of supply and demand

D) An increasing opportunity cost

Business corporations promote fair competition for the benefit of consumers. This is regulated by the United States **antitrust law**, which is a collection of state and federal government laws.

Which of the following depicts the main purpose of the antitrust law?

A) Help businesses that are in financial trouble

B) Prevent business behavior that hampers competition

C) Establish trust between government and businesses

D) Encourage business investment

## 46

A horizontal analysis involves comparing ratios or line items in a company's financial statements over a certain period.

Which of the following is essential in the identification of trends in financial data for a horizontal analysis?

A) Data from a zero-based budget

B) Data in financial reports from multiple time periods

C) Data from the most recent financial report

D) Data in a Statement of Cash Flows

CONTINUE ▶

47

Production is a process of workers' mixing different material and immaterial inputs to obtain a product for consumption.

Is the production involved in businesses like banks and dry cleaners?

A) Yes, these businesses manufacture a line of tangible products.

B) Yes, services rendered by these businesses serves as their products.

C) No, these businesses do not involve production.

D) No, services rendered by these businesses are intangible.

48

Cost analysis involves estimation of an alternatives' strengths and weakness.

In which of the following situations would a firm use the cost analysis?

A) To evaluate the amount of money associated with inventory storage.

B) To predict sales volume for a specified period.

C) To determine the number of delinquent accounts.

D) To assess income changes over a specified period.

49

Compensation can be defined as a systematic approach in giving monetary value to employees in exchange for their work.

Which of the following compensations would have the highest positive effect on a worker's productivity and motivation?

A) Give a regularly scheduled salary increase.

B) Give a high pay level as the beginning salary.

C) Increase the pay of senior employees.

D) A varied and attainable pay mix.

50

Which of the following situations does not establish the scarcity of a certain good?

A) It is readily available in the market.

B) It has a shortage at some positive price.

C) It has many stocks in the marketplace.

D) It can be bought as many as possible at its current market price.

51

An **opportunity cost** is commonly defined as the loss of potential gain from other alternatives when another alternative is chosen.

Which of the following is another definition of opportunity cost?

A) It is the cost incurred by producing the most demanded goods.

B) It is the cost that will maximize the highest profit for a given company.

C) It is the cost of one product or service that must be given up in exchange for the production of an additional unit of another product.

D) It is the total labor cost of producing goods.

52

Ticker symbol is a type of shorthand used for the names of a company.

Which of the following is true regarding ticker symbols?

A) It tells what kind of stock it is.

B) Only the companies on New York Stock Exchange is given this symbol.

C) It can uniquely identify a company.

D) It is composed of the company name's first three letters.

53

Debt financing is the act of acquiring money from an outside party with an agreement that the payment of the initial principal would have a negotiated level of interest.

Which of the following is a good example of debt financing for raising capital?

A) Promissory notes

B) Initial public offerings

C) Direct stock offerings

D) Convertible securities

54

A finance charge is any fee that denotes the credit cost, or the cost of borrowing.

Which of the following expresses finance charges?

A) Monthly balance rate

B) Annual percentage rate

C) Monthly percentage rate

D) Annual balance rate

Number of Workers	Total Output of Oil
0	0
1	25
2	44
3	60
4	70
5	75

The table given above shows the relationship between the number of workers and oil output (in tons per day) of a particular oil company.

Suppose that $5.00 per ton is charged for and the wage rate is $40.00 per day.

How many workers should the oil company hire?

A) 6

B) 4

C) 2

D) 1

Prepaid insurance reports the cost of the insurance contract wherein a prior payment has been made.

What part of a balance sheet is the prepaid insurance recorded?

A) Assets

B) Equity

C) Expenses

D) Liability

57

In economics, **inflation** is defined as the sustained increase in the price level of goods and services over a period.

What type of inflation would happen in case of price level elevation due to rise in the cost of raw materials?

A) Demand-pull inflation
B) Hyperinflation
C) Cost-push inflation
D) Deflation

58

Increase in product sales by one unit generates an additional revenue called the **marginal revenue**.

If the total revenue increases along with the output increase, what will happen to the marginal revenue?

A) It will be decreasing.
B) It will be equal to the average revenue.
C) It will be less than the average revenue.
D) It will be greater than zero.

59

A **standard of living** refers to the extent of wealth, comfort, goods as well as necessities that is accessible to a socioeconomic class or a geographic area.

Which of the following results in a higher standard of living in a country?

A) When productivity increases at a rate faster than the population.
B) When productivity and population increase at the same rate.
C) When productivity decreases while the population remains the same.
D) When the productivity remains the same while the population increases.

60

During recession (a period of temporary economic decline), trade and industrial activity are reduced, identified generally by a fall in GDP in two successive quarters.

Which of the following options is attributed to the unemployment rate during this time?

A) It is less than the natural unemployment rate.
B) It is less than the growth rate of the economy.
C) It is equal to the natural rate of unemployment.
D) It is greater than the natural rate of unemployment.

CONTINUE ▶

61

Which of the following is a common problem in financial information management?

A) There are insufficiency in financial information becuase of compliance regulations.

B) Concerning financial data, there is too much dependence on the master source and system.

C) Many financial data sources and systems are present within an organization.

D) There is a strict compliance in terms of data governance policies and processes.

62

If there is an increase in the output produced, which of the following costs must decrease continuously in a short period?

A) The total fixed cost of producing goods.

B) The total variable cost of producing goods and services.

C) The average total cost of producing goods.

D) The average fixed cost of producing goods.

63

A particular company uses only labor and capital in its production process.

Which would most likely be the optimal combination of inputs for the company in the long run?

A) The marginal product per dollar spent on capital is equal to the marginal product per dollar spent on labor.

B) All average products are equal to all marginal products.

C) The total product of capital is equal to the total product of labor.

D) The marginal product of capital is equal to the marginal product of labor.

64

One reason a business analyzes financial data is to make decisions that may affect the business' welfare.

Which of the following is an example of this action?

A) To be able to prepare the company's tax return, Aurora obtains the necessary financial documents and forms.

B) Tamara orders the staff accountant to prepare the company's profit-and-loss statement for the executive board meeting.

C) Upon review of the sales forecasts and income statements, Abby identified that the company has enough budget for hiring a new employee.

D) June gets a copy of the business's credit rating report from a credit bureau.

65

Which of the following cases exhibits characteristics of an oligopolistic market?

A) The sellers have no competition in the market trading.

B) There are many sellers having the same products and have no barriers to entry.

C) There are only a few competing sellers having similar products and have high barriers to entry.

D) There are many sellers, with each having unique products and have no barriers to entry.

66

The cost of grapes has been in equilibrium. Which factors would most likely influence the price equilibrium of grapes to decline?

A) A fungus is spreading through grapes farms.

B) A number of substitutes for grapes has significantly increased their costs.

C) Studies show that grapes have traces of cancer-causing substances procured from pesticides.

D) Significant weather disturbances frequently occur during this grape-growing season.

67

Which of the following insurance coverage would be the most appropriate for a newly hired employee who starts in a month but saves money to buy a car, and is currently using bus transportation since he lives near a bus line?

A) Renter's insurance and COBRA

B) Renter's insurance and temporary short-term health insurance

C) Auto insurance and temporary short-term health insurance

D) Health and life insurance

68

One type of insurance company, the **risk retention group**, is owned by its members or its stockholders.

Which of the following statements is correct about the risk retention group?

A) Compared with the traditional insurance companies, higher licensing fees are paid by the risk retention group.

B) The risks are regulated by the group members by retainment of equity and transfer of liabilities to external sources.

C) Companies from different industries may be insured by the same risk retention group.

D) The policyholders of a risk retention group are also its stockholders.

69

The merging of financial providers that are on the same institutional category is called **consolidation**.

Which of the following do financial firms want to achieve when they consolidate?

A) To have fewer assets
B) To have fewer products
C) To lower the risks
D) To lower the costs

70

Which of the following is the main reason why businesses utilize data mining techniques to gather various types of financial information?

A) Identifying the relationships and patterns among data.
B) Effectively managing their working capital.
C) Analyzing the accuracy of their accounting records.
D) Developing their financial goals.

71

What is the primary reason why the use of online technology has increased in financial-information management?

A) The customer's right to privacy is protected.
B) Electronic documents are recognized as legally binding by passages of laws.
C) The electronic information exchange procedures are removed.
D) Recognizing that security of transactions is not considered as an issue.

72

Financial assets or the financial value of assets are considered as capitals.

Which of the following is the common means of finance for companies in raising their capital?

A) Invest deposits from savers
B) Invest funds from premium payments
C) Establish mutual funds and investment banks
D) Issue notes, bonds, and other obligations

73

Financial services include a wide range of businesses that involve managing money.

Which of the following statements is not correct about working in the financial services industry?

A) The financial-services industry includes fund managers, real estate brokers, and auditors.

B) Financial services professionals can typically earn above-average salaries.

C) An individual working in financial services is limited to work at an investment firm, a bank, or an insurance company.

D) Financial services professionals are present in all kinds of companies, from large corporations to sole proprietorships.

74

Finance professional provides guidance concerning investment decisions.

Which of the following should a finance professional be capable of by analyzing a customer's financial information?

A) Identifying the customer's newest target market.

B) Declaring Chapter 11 bankruptcy for the customer.

C) Protecting the security of financial information of the customer.

D) Developing a financial strategy to help the customer.

75

Rather than accepting a job that offered an annual salary of $14,000, Jenna opted to enroll instead in a two-year program at the local community college.

How much would the opportunity cost of attending the community college be if the annual tuition fees are $5,400?

A) $5,400

B) $8,600

C) $14,000

D) $19,400

76

Which of the following results from management of budgeting data efficiently by means of budgeting applications?

A) The management's confidence in their budget increases.

B) The need for having an audit trail decreases.

C) The amount of time needed to be spent on value-added activities increases.

D) The auditors' ability to trace the numbers used in budgets decreases.

Suppose that cereals and breads are substitutes.

What will most likely happen if there is a significant decrease in the supply of cereals in the market?

A) There will be an increased demand on the supply of breads.
B) There will be an increased demand for breads, and therefore, its price will also increase.
C) There will be a decline in the demand for breads, and therefore, its price will also decrease.
D) There will be a decline in the supply of breads, and therefore, its price will decrease.

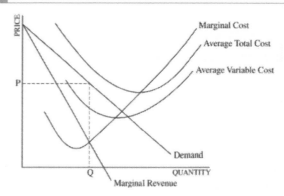

The graph above shows Company Z's profit-maximizing performance.

What can be inferred from the graph shown above?

A) Company Z should exit if conditions do not improve in the long run.
B) Company Z should increase output production to maximize profits.
C) Company Z should increase the price to maximize profits.
D) Company Z should produce the output that minimizes average total cost.

79

The production process of a U.S. textile company displays economies of scale.

Which of the following will most likely occur if the company increases its output?

A) There will be an increase in the long-run average total costs of the company.

B) There will be a decline in the short-run total costs of the company.

C) There will be a decline in the long-run average total costs of the company.

D) There will be an increase in the short-run average total costs of the company.

80

A retail store specializes in leather garments. Under normal circumstances, the supply stock raises proportionally with the quantity and price, while the demand decreases proportionally with the quantity and price.

What effect would a simultaneous increase in the amount of leather and consumers' incomes have on the price and quantity?

A) Increase in price, indeterminate quantity

B) Increase in price, increase in quantity

C) Indeterminate price, decrease in quantity

D) Decrease in price, decrease in quantity

81

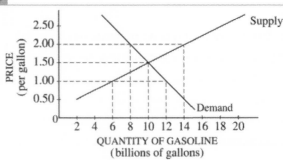

Given the diagram above, which of the following will most likely happen if the government imposes a ceiling price of $1.00 per gallon of gasoline?

A) There will be a shortage of 12 billion gallons of gasoline in the market.

B) There will be a shortage of 6 billion gallons of gasoline in the market.

C) There will be a surplus production of 12 billion gallons of gasoline.

D) There will be a surplus production of 6 billion gallons of gasoline.

82

Fiscal policy refers to the government's utilization of its revenue collection mostly taxes, as well as expenditures, to influence the country's economy.

Which of the following options would be found during a recession?

A) A decrease in the discount rate

B) A decrease in the reserve requirement

C) An increase in government spending

D) An increase in taxes

CONTINUE ▶

83

A bank receives a cash deposit from a new customer amounting to $500; however it is currently fully loaned up.

If the required reserve ratio is 20%, which of the following options is the bank required to do?

A) Lend 20% of the $500 and keep the rest as reserves.

B) Send 80% of the $500 to the Federal Reserve Bank.

C) Keep 20% of the $500 as reserves.

D) Keep 80% of the $500 as reserves.

84

In regards to finance, **private equity secondary market** refers to the buying and selling of pre-existing investor commitments to private equity as well as other alternative investment funds.

Which of the following options depicts what would happen to the private market if a good generates negative externalities?

A) Under-produce goods relative to the socially optimal level of output

B) Charge lower than the market equilibrium price to compensate for the externality

C) The goods will be overproduced relative to the level of output that is considered socially optimal.

D) Compensate the third parties harmed by the negative externality

CONTINUE ▶

85

A dairy products company, Company X, is in a constant-cost, perfectly competitive long-run equilibrium.

If there is an increase in the number of consumers for dairy products, what will be the most likely effect of it on Company X?

A) There will be an upward shift in all short-run cost curves of Company X, followed by a higher long-run price for dairy products.

B) Some dairy companies will close, and Company X's short-run profits will be reduced.

C) The dairy products will have higher short-run and long-run prices.

D) There will be a higher short-run price for dairy products, followed by an increase in the quantity produced.

86

In economics, business expenses independent on the level of goods or services produced by the business are fixed costs, indirect costs or overheads.

Which of the following fixed cost options can be found in the case of a bakery?

A) Fuel costs for operating its delivery trucks.

B) The price of flour and sugar.

C) Wage payments to its workers.

D) Monthly rental payments on the building it occupies.

87

During a week, a person consumes only two types of goods, noted as M and N, and spends his whole income on these, while the marginal utility of the last dollar spent on good M being 5 and the marginal utility of the last dollar spent on good N is 10.

Which of the following this person does to maximize his utility?

A) Buy fewer units of M and more units of N.

B) Buy fewer units of N and more units of M.

C) Buy fewer units of both M and N.

D) Maintain current consumption level of the two goods.

88

Producing a particular type of good causes a positive externality.

In what way can the government increase the allocative efficiency of the production of such good?

A) Imposing a price floor to decrease production

B) Subsidizing the good producer

C) Increasing the tax of the good producer

D) Imposing a price ceiling to increase production

89

In cases where a specific person or enterprise is the only supplier of a specific commodity, monopoly exists.

Which of the following is not a characteristic of monopoly?

A) Only one firm is selling a particular product.

B) The commodities are charged a price below average variable cost to maximize profit.

C) It has a downward-sloping demand curve.

D) The primary goal is to maximize profit.

90

Command economy or **administrative command economy** is an economy wherein the government plays a central role in directing the allocation of resources in these economic systems, as opposed to planned coordination.

Which of the following manages resource allocations in a command economy?

A) Central planning

B) Competitive markets

C) Labor unions

D) Large corporations

91

Marginal propensity to consume (MPC) is a component of the Keynesian macroeconomic theory.

Which of the following ratios is MPC measured as?

A) The ratio of equilibrium income to the total consumption.

B) The ratio of total consumption to the total disposable income.

C) The ratio of change in consumption to the change in disposable income.

D) The ratio of change in equilibrium income to the change in investment spending.

92

Regarding economics, **a public good** is defined as a commodity or service that is non-excludable, non-rivalrous, and where consumption by an individual does not reduce availability to others.

Which of the following best depicts the term "nonrival" in this case?

A) Free riders mostly consume the public good.

B) The public product is provided at zero marginal cost.

C) The government produced public good, without any competition.

D) An individual's consumption of the public good does not reduce the amount available to others.

93

Suppose that labor and land, whose prices are constant, are the inputs of Mr. Johnson in farming corn. After several cycles of harvest seasons, he observed that if the inputs are doubled, the quantity of corn produced doubles.

Based on this situation, which of the following is true regarding Mr. Johnson's long-run average total cost curve?

A) Sloping upward
B) Sloping downward
C) Vertically oriented
D) Horizontally oriented

94

Assume that the majority of Americans prefer tomatoes on their hamburgers.

Which scenario will most likely to happen if there is a decrease in the supply of hamburgers?

A) There will be an increase in the demand for tomatoes because tomatoes are substitutes for hamburgers.
B) There will be no effect on the demand for tomatoes because hamburgers and tomatoes are independent goods.
C) There will be an increase in the demand for tomatoes because tomatoes and hamburgers are complements.
D) There will be a decline in the demand for tomatoes because tomatoes and hamburgers are complements.

95

Which of the following conditions given below can result in a profit-maximizing company to shut down production to minimize short-run losses?

A) The total cost is higher than the total revenue.
B) The average total cost is less than the marginal cost.
C) The marginal revenue is higher than the marginal cost.
D) The average variable cost is greater than the average revenue.

96

The cost of the goods or services must lie between the opportunity costs of producers involved in the trade for it to be mutually beneficial among each party involved. This occurs when the opportunity cost ratios for two individuals performing particular tasks differ.

Which of the following is an economic term that refers to an economy's ability to produce goods and services at a lower opportunity cost than that of trade partners?

A) Absolute advantage
B) Comparative advantage
C) Price elasticity
D) Market equilibrium

97

A sales team has discovered that pricing their product $8 per unit yields 400 buyers, on the other hand, pricing their product $4 per unit will yield 800 buyers.

Which type of demand is expressed by the price elasticity given above?

A) Inelastic

B) Perfectly inelastic

C) Unit elastic

D) Elastic

98

The pollution level generated by companies contribute to a part of their total tax.

Which of the following would most likely be the effect of this policy?

A) As the production increases, the pollution produced increases.

B) As the production increases, the pollution produced decreases.

C) As the production decreases, the pollution produced increases.

D) As the production decreases, the pollution produced decreases.

99

Suppose that only two goods are produced by both Norway and Scotland which are cheese and milk. Between these countries, Norway has a comparative advantage in cheese production.

Which of the following statements is correct based on the situation given above?

A) Norway must hold an absolute advantage in the production of cheese.

B) Scotland holds a comparative advantage in the production of milk.

C) Norway's opportunity cost of producing one additional unit of cheese is lower than Scotland's.

D) Scotland's opportunity cost of producing one additional unit of milk is lower than Norway's

100

The macroeconomic measure of the value of economic output adjusted for changes in price is the **Real Gross Domestic Product** (real GDP). Nominal GDP is GDP evaluated at current market prices.

Which of the following measures the ratio of nominal GDP to the real GDP?

A) GDP deflator

B) Money supply

C) Government's budget deficit

D) Unemployment rate

A **monopoly market** involves a single seller selling a unique product without competition as it is the sole seller of that specific product.

Which of the following would explain the inefficiency of a monopoly market structure?

A) In a monopoly company, too many profits will be earned.

B) In a monopoly economy, there is too little production output, and a price above marginal cost would be set.

C) In a monopoly economy, the products produced are not government-regulated.

D) In a monopoly economy, there is no incentive to minimize its cost.

Which of the following statements illustrates the law of diminishing marginal utility?

A) As more units of Product A are consumed, the total satisfaction declines.

B) As consumption of Product A increases, the additional satisfaction obtained from consuming extra units of Product A declines.

C) As consumption of Product A decreases, the additional satisfaction obtained from consuming extra units of Product A declines.

D) The total utility decreases when marginal utility declines.

Monopoly is a market situation that involves a single producer in charge on controling the supply of goods.

Which condition is consistent with the conditions of a natural monopoly?

A) As output increases, the long-run total cost decreases.

B) The long-run average total cost remains constant while the output is increasing.

C) As output increases, the long-run average total cost decreases.

D) Profits will be maximized by setting price and marginal cost equal.

Company K has newly opened a branch and begins to hire workers for its new branch with a fixed amount of machinery.

What would most likely happen to the marginal product when the company hires additional workers?

A) The marginal product will initially decline, but will then eventually rise.

B) The marginal product will initially rise, but will then eventually fall.

C) The marginal product will rise consistently due to the diminishing return.

D) The marginal product will decline consistently due to the division of labor.

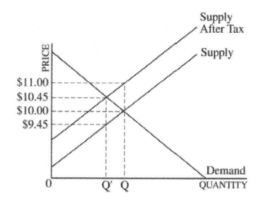

Given the diagram above, which of the following would be the amount of unit tax?

A) $0.50

B) $0.45

C) $1.45

D) $1.00

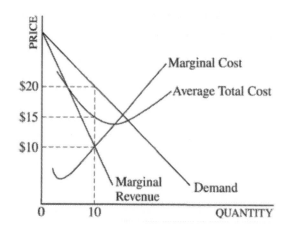

Suppose that a company increases its production beyond ten units.

Which of the statements would most likely occur?

A) Charging $20 per unit will attract customers to buy more than ten units.

B) The company's profits will rapidly increase.

C) The company will lower its price to sell more than ten units.

D) The company will lose a lot of profit.

In economic analysis, **derived demand** is a term used to describe a demand placed on one good or service resulting from the price for some other related goods or services.

Which of the following options describes best why the demand for labor is also known as derived demand?

A) It is directly related to the marginal utility of working

B) It is inversely related to the wage rate

C) It is dependant on the availability of capital goods

D) It is dependant on demand for the final product that the labor is used to produce

A significant portion of potato crops has been damaged by intense drought; however, there is a rise in the revenues of potato farmers.

What can we infer from the situation stated above?

A) The supply for potatoes is unit price inelastic.

B) The demand for potatoes is price elastic.

C) The demand for potatoes is unit price inelastic.

D) The demand for potatoes is unit price elastic.

A company exhibits a constant-cost perfectly competitive performance in the long-run equilibrium.

Which of the statements given below correctly describes this company?

A) An increase in the demand of the company's product will result in no change in the long-run equilibrium price of the product.

B) A decrease in the demand of the company's product will result in no change in the long-run equilibrium quantity of the product.

C) The long-run demand curve is downward sloping.

D) The total cost of production increases as the number of product increases.

One of the primary basic models discussed in economics is the circular-flow model. This model describes the flow of money and products throughout the economy in a very simplified manner.

Which of the following best describes the roles of firms and households in the product markets and factor markets?

A) Product markets: firms buy goods from households; Factor market: firms purchase resources from households

B) Product markets: firms buy goods from households; Factor market: firms sell resources to households

C) Product markets: firms sell goods to households; Factor market: firms sell resources to households

D) Product markets: firms sell goods to households; Factor market: firms buy resources from households

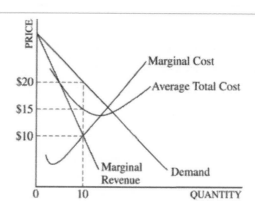

Given the diagram above, which would most likely happen to the economic profit of a company if it produces ten units of product?

A) It will be equal to $250.

B) It will be equal to $50.

C) It will be equal to $150.

D) It will be less than $50.

Severe weather conditions are being experienced by certain cities resulting in a prolonged outage. As a result, high demands for flashlight has significantly increased its price making the cities' officials pass laws that prohibit price increase in flashlights.

Which of the following would most likely be the effect of passing such laws?

A) More flashlights will be available in the market.

B) There will be a shortage of flashlights in the market.

C) The supply curve for flashlights will shift to the right.

D) The availability of flashlights in the market will not be affected.

SECTION 6 ECONOMICS & FINANCE

#	Answer	Topic	Subtopic	#	Answer	Topic	Subtopic	#	Answer	Topic	Subtopic	#	Answer	Topic	Subtopic
1	B	TB	S2	29	C	TB	S2	57	C	TB	S1	85	D	TB	S1
2	B	TB	S2	30	A	TB	S2	58	D	TB	S1	86	D	TB	S1
3	D	TB	S2	31	C	TB	S2	59	A	TB	S2	87	A	TB	S1
4	B	TB	S2	32	B	TB	S2	60	D	TB	S1	88	B	TB	S1
5	D	TB	S2	33	D	TB	S1	61	C	TB	S2	89	B	TB	S1
6	A	TB	S1	34	B	TB	S2	62	D	TB	S1	90	A	TB	S1
7	C	TB	S2	35	D	TB	S2	63	A	TB	S1	91	C	TB	S1
8	D	TB	S2	36	A	TB	S2	64	C	TB	S2	92	D	TB	S1
9	A	TB	S2	37	C	TB	S2	65	C	TB	S1	93	B	TB	S1
10	B	TB	S2	38	C	TB	S2	66	C	TB	S1	94	D	TB	S1
11	B	TB	S1	39	A	TB	S1	67	C	TB	S2	95	D	TB	S1
12	B	TB	S2	40	D	TB	S2	68	D	TB	S2	96	B	TB	S1
13	B	TB	S2	41	D	TB	S2	69	D	TB	S2	97	C	TB	S1
14	D	TB	S1	42	D	TB	S2	70	A	TB	S2	98	D	TB	S1
15	C	TB	S2	43	D	TB	S2	71	B	TB	S2	99	A	TB	S1
16	A	TB	S2	44	D	TB	S1	72	D	TB	S2	100	A	TB	S1
17	A	TB	S2	45	B	TB	S1	73	C	TB	S2	101	B	TB	S1
18	D	TB	S1	46	B	TB	S2	74	D	TB	S2	102	B	TB	S1
19	C	TB	S2	47	B	TB	S2	75	D	TB	S1	103	C	TB	S1
20	D	TB	S2	48	A	TB	S2	76	A	TB	S2	104	B	TB	S1
21	A	TB	S2	49	D	TB	S2	77	B	TB	S1	105	D	TB	S1
22	B	TB	S2	50	A	TB	S1	78	A	TB	S1	106	C	TB	S1
23	D	TB	S2	51	C	TB	S1	79	C	TB	S1	107	D	TB	S1
24	B	TB	S2	52	C	TB	S2	80	A	TB	S1	108	C	TB	S1
25	B	TB	S1	53	A	TB	S2	81	B	TB	S1	109	A	TB	S1
26	D	TB	S1	54	B	TB	S2	82	C	TB	S1	110	D	TB	S1
27	C	TB	S2	55	B	TB	S1	83	C	TB	S1	111	B	TB	S1
28	A	TB	S1	56	A	TB	S2	84	C	TB	S1	112	B	TB	S1

Topics & Subtopics

Code	Description	Code	Description
SB1	Economics	TB	Business Basics
SB2	Finance		

CONTINUE ▶

TEST DIRECTION

DIRECTIONS

Read the questions carefully and then choose the ONE best answer to each question.

Be sure to allocate your time carefully so you are able to complete the entire test within the testing session. You may go back and review your answers at any time.

You may use any available space in your test booklet for scratch work.

Questions in this booklet are not actual test questions but they are the samples for commonly asked questions.

This test aims to cover all topics which may appear on the actual test. However some topics may not be covered.

Studying this booklet will be preparing you for the actual test. It will not guarantee improving your test score but it will help you pass your exam on the first attempt.

Some useful tips for answering multiple choice questions;

- Start with the questions that you can easily answer.

- Underline the keywords in the question.

- Be sure to read all the choices given.

- Watch for keywords such as NOT, always, only, all, never, completely.

- Do not forget to answer every question.

CONTINUE ▶

1

Data mining is a computing process that involves going through large data sets to discover patterns and is used by companies to obtain useful information from raw data.

Which of the following best describes Weblog data mining?

A) Designing a collection of interlinked electronic documents.

B) Managing risk associated with Web server activity.

C) Automatically analyzing customer activity on a Weblog.

D) Storing a company's historical data.

2

How much is the net income or net loss of a business owner if her initial and final capital is $25,000 and $37,000, respectively, while her withdrawals amounted to $23,000?

A) Net loss of $35,000

B) Net loss of $14,000

C) Net income of $35,000

D) Net loss of $14,000

3

What is the Consumer Price Index (CPI)?

A) It is an advance projection of the average per capita cost of goods and services of food industries.

B) It is the annual average per capita expenditure on food production services.

C) It is a measure of the average change in prices over time for specific goods or services.

D) It is the annual average per capita expenditure on food.

4

What is the basic concept of marketing?

A) Drafting strategies to hire and train competent and capable sales staff.

B) Constructing processes to increase the efficiency of the production and allocation of goods.

C) Implementing procedures to help potential customers in getting their needs and wants.

D) Designating a fixed percentage of revenues for the promotion of the products to consumers.

Trade, or commerce, refers to the transfer of goods or services between individuals often in exchange for money.

Which of the following should one country possess for a trade to exist between two countries?

A) Joint venture
B) Opportunity cost
C) Export quota
D) Comparative advantage

Profitability is the degree by which a business or an activity obtains a profit or a financial gain. It is also the metric used for determining the extent of a company's profit in regards to the size of the business.

Which of the following best describes a measure of profitability?

A) Working capital
B) Return on assets ratio
C) Debt to total assets ratio
D) Current ratio

A business cycle consists of different phases. Which phase is a company currently in, if it experiences high levels of business failures as well as unemployment?

A) Peak
B) Recovery
C) Expansion
D) Trough

Accounting form is a combination of accounting registers and the manner in which economic transactions are recorded and reported.

Which of the following is the source of information used to journalize adjusting entries?

A) Balance sheet
B) Work sheet
C) Income statement
D) Trial balance

9

A retail store agrees to share the advertising costs of a product with the product's national distributor.

Which type of advertising is this retail store planning to do?

A) National advertising
B) Trade advertising
C) Industrial advertising
D) Cooperative advertising

10

Which of the following refers to the process that involves maintaining a running account of the merchandise on hand?

A) Perpetual inventory
B) Book inventory
C) Physical inventory
D) Economic order quantity

11

If a lending company is to review a borrower's accounting documentation, which of the following undergoes evaluation?

A) The creditworthiness.
B) The current assets to past liabilities.
C) The expenses concerning employee risk management.
D) The aggregate statistics relating to the probability that a competitor will enter.

12

What is the markup percentage of a cookware set if it has a retail cost of $40 but its actual value was $25?

A) 25%
B) 37.5%
C) 60%
D) 75%

13

Which of the following terms refers to the difference between the balance of a plant asset account and related accumulated depreciation account?

A) Book value
B) Liability
C) Market value
D) Contra asset

14

How frequent should an accountant prepare an income statement when a company is aiming to regulate its spending and track incoming funds?

A) Every year
B) Every six (6) months
C) Every two (2) months
D) Every month

15

Which of the following accounting assumptions indicates that an enterprise will continuously operate long enough to carry out its current goals and commitments?

A) Time period assumption

B) Going concern assumption

C) Economic entity assumption

D) Operation assumption

16

A bank is currently fully loaned up. However, the bank received a $500 cash deposit from its new customer.

If the required reserve ratio is 20%, which of the following is the maximum increase in the money supply that can be made from the deposit?

A) $2,500

B) $2,000

C) $400

D) $500

17

An accountant in a company is deciding whether to record a sale upon the receipt of the order for services or upon the completion of the services.

Which of the following issues can the situation be considered as?

A) A communicaton issue

B) A classification issue

C) A valuation issue

D) A recognition issue

18

Which of the following refers to the process that involves marketing and selling of products directly to the home of the consumers?

A) Consignment

B) Merchandising

C) Direct selling

D) Comparison shopping

CONTINUE ▶

19

It is the paid mention of a company, product, or service by a form of media.

Which of the following terms is being referred to by the preceding sentence given above?

A) Advertising

B) Puffing

C) Public relations

D) Third-party endorsement

20

In opening multiple businesses, which of the following is the most vital business activities to consider first?

A) Accounting

B) Management

C) Production

D) Marketing

21

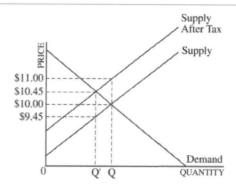

Based on the diagram above, how much does the customer pay and how much does the producer receive after deducting tax?

A) The customer pays $11.00, and the producer will receive $10.45.

B) The customer pays $11.00, and the producer will receive $10.00.

C) The customer pays $10.45, and the producer will receive $10.00.

D) The customer pays $10.45, and the producer will receive $9.45.

22

Which strategy is frequently adopted by firms that view themselves as market leaders in product quality?

A) The strategy to expand the overall market

B) Market share strategy

C) The strategy that focuses on non-price benefits

D) Penetration pricing strategy

23

A business has a list consisting of the merchandise lines carried, as well as the depth and breadth in which the products are stocked.

Which of the following terms refers to the listing mentioned above?

A) Buying plan
B) Price-line list
C) Merchandise mix
D) Basic stock list

24

In a **free enterprise**, the products, services as well as prices are determined by the market and not the government.

Which of the following also refers to a free enterprise system?

A) Socialism
B) Monopoly
C) Democracy
D) Capitalism

25

Which of the following is the main difference between the cost and accrual accounting systems in relation to recording business transactions?

A) Scope
B) Timing
C) Complexity
D) Frequency

26

When purchasing a product, a **coupon** is a ticket used to redeem a financial discount or rebate.

What is a coupon called when it is included in a package for later purchase?

A) Rebate coupon
B) Free-standing coupon
C) Bounce-back coupon
D) Instant-redemption coupon

27

Which of the following statements accurately defines working capital?

A) It is a measure of profitability.
B) It is a measure of consistency.
C) It is a measure of liquidity.
D) It is a measure of solvency.

28

A company started the accounting period with an initial of $50,000 in the owner's capital and a final of $75,000.

What would be the company's net income or loss for the period given above if there is also a withdrawals of $30,000 during the period?

A) $30,000 net loss

B) $5,000 net loss

C) $55,000 net income

D) $5,000 net income

29

Prepaid Income refers to a payment that has been received prior to the delivery of a service or goods.

Which of the following is a prepaid income account?

A) Fixed asset

B) Current asset

C) Revenue

D) Liability

30

When buying an office building, which of the following should a long-term note payable be reported as?

A) A noncash investing and financing activity

B) Cash outflow in the operating section of the cash flow statement

C) Cash outflow in the investing section of the cash flow statement

D) Cash outflow in the financing section of the cash flow statement

31

Publicity involves the giving out of information about a product, person, or company for advertising or promotional purposes.

Which of the following is developed by a business in seeking publicity?

A) A positive perception of the business.

B) Establish a connection with potential customers.

C) Awareness of the business's products or services.

D) A working relationship with the media.

32

An **income statement** is a financial statement reporting the financial performance of a company over a specific accounting period.

Which of the following options given below cannot be found on an income statement?

A) Cash

B) Sale Revenues

C) Interest Income

D) Insurance Expense

33

During the year, Eric's Car Repair Shop accumulated $100,000 in car repair revenues, spent $55,000 in expenses and $10,000 dividends.

If the shop started the year initially with total assets of $60,000 and total liabilities of $40,000, what is the net income of the car repair shop for the year?

A) $45,000

B) $20,000

C) $90,000

D) $35,000

34

A type of financial statement summarizing a company's assets, liabilities and shareholders' equity at a specific point in time is called a **balance sheet**.

Which of the following given below can be found on a balance sheet?

A) Interest Income

B) Inventory

C) Cost of Goods Sold

D) Sales

35

A company's accounts receivable balance is $30,000 at the beginning of June and $25,000 at the end of June. On the other hand, their total sales for the month amounted to $530,000.

Which of the following is the correct amount of money gathered from sales for the month of June?

A) $515,000

B) $535,000

C) $545,000

D) None of the above.

36

Prior to the launch of a new and unique product to the market, which of the following is the most appropriate pricing strategy a company should use?

A) Price skimming

B) Penetration pricing

C) Promotional pricing

D) Psychological pricing

37

Given that a Sam's account is being written off during a specified period, but he signed a check for $2,000 at the same period.

How should this transaction be recorded in the books of the company that received the money from Sam?

A) Debit Accounts – Receivable $2,000 and Credit Cash – $2,000

B) Debit Cash – $2,000 and Credit Accounts Receivable – $2,000

C) Debit Cash – $2,000 and Credit Allowance for Bad Debts – $2,000

D) Debit Cash – $2,000 and Credit Bad Debts Expense – $2,000

38

The cost layering methods, **FIFO** and **LIFO**, are used to value the cost of goods sold and ending inventory.

In the case of price increases over time, which of the following options would lead to an increase in the sales cost?

A) Both FIFO and LIFO.

B) "First in, First Out" (FIFO)

C) "Last in, First Out" (LIFO)

D) None of the above.

39

The medium used for exchanging for goods or services within an economy is the **currency**.

Which of the following significantly affects the value of a nation's currency?

A) CPI, Immigration, Unemployment rate, and Job Availability.

B) The unemployment rate, job availability, Imports, and Exports.

C) GDP, Imports, Exports, and CPI.

D) Imports, GDP, Immigration, and Unemployment Rate.

40

Team selling is a strategy that involves groups of individuals working together towards a common sales goal.

Which of the following options is the main objective of team-based selling?

A) To match different functional areas of the company with the customer needs

B) To equitably manage the sales bonus pool

C) To make multiple points of contact between the customer and the company

D) To distribute the work involved in managing an account

41

Which of the following refers to anything, which can be a design, sign, or expression, that is easily recognizable and be associated with the products or services of a particular company, providing them exclusive rights by law to use a brand?

A) Trade name
B) Brand loyalty
C) Brand mark
D) Trademark

42

Which of the following strategies in pricing aims to make a product's price more attractive by affecting the customer's judgment of price?

A) Markup pricing
B) Captive pricing
C) Demand-based pricing
D) Psychological pricing

43

Operating expenses are the expenses from activities that are not directly related with the primary operation of a business, such as production or sales.

Which of the following would not be considered as an operating expense for a retailer?

A) Property taxes
B) Salaries
C) Interest on loans
D) All of the above

44

Which of the following is defined as the process of making a salesperson do many unsolicited sales calls to possible customers he does not know?

A) Sales-associate method
B) Cold canvassing
C) Multilevel marketing
D) Center-of-Influence method

45

A **complementary relationship** is a mutual affinity where the participants with different behavior patterns do what is in joint interest and sustain the relationship.

Which of the following shows a complementary relationship?

A) Ground coffee and tea
B) Peanut butter and jelly
C) Mechanical pencils and pens
D) Synthetic oil and batteries

46

Point of sale (POS) is the area of a store where customers can pay for their purchases. A company decided to purchase a POS cash register on the 1st of January for $5,400 which has a useful life of ten years.

The double declining balance method of depreciation is a form of accelerated depreciation which has a depreciation rate of two times the straight-line depreciation rate.

Using the double-declining-balance method, what would be the value of the depreciation expense for the second year of its useful life?

A) $800
B) $500
C) $1,000
D) $864

47

One of the best catering providers in the country is the Griffins Company. They currently signed a 5-year contract that provided full payment for a check worth $800,000.

Which of the following accounts will record the payment received if the company uses the cash basis of accounting?

A) Service Revenue
B) Unearned Revenue
C) Prepaid Expense
D) Accounts Payable

CONTINUE ▶

48

A survey is conducted by a marketing researcher in a large selling area, but gathers only a small group of people to serve as representatives of all the people in that area.

Which of the following term describes this group of representative people?

A) Universe

B) Sample

C) Population

D) Stratification

49

The expenses are matched with the related revenues upon expiry or transfer of title to a buyer and not upon payment of the expenses. This occurs under the **accrual basis of accounting**.

Which of the following is an example of this type of accounting?

A) Recognizing that prepaid insurance is an asset.

B) Recognizing interest income after receiving it.

C) Verifying that assets are equal to liabilities owner's equity.

D) Putting someone in charge of preparing a list of the received checks and someone else in charge of depositing them.

50

Statement of cash flows is a financial statement summary that provides an overview of a business' cash inflows and outflows for a specific duration of time.

Which of the following is not an activity listed in the statement of cash flows?

A) Financing Activities

B) Operating Activities

C) Investing Activities

D) Funding Activities

51

An **advertisement** is a material shown to the public to promote a product, service, or event or even publicize a job vacancy.

Which of the following advertisements shows a celebrity encouraging children to eat fresh fruits and vegetables?

A) Reminder advertising

B) Public service announcement

C) Word of mouth

D) Product-focused advertising

52

Production-related materials are those items classified as material purchases and included in the Cost of Goods Sold as raw material purchases.

Which of the following describes an Italian company selling production materials to a company based in the United States?

A) The inventory manager

B) A part of the supply chain

C) The manufacturing agent

D) A distribution center

53

Advertising campaign involves an organized course of action done for the promotion of a product or service.

Which of the following options is the first step in initiating a new advertising campaign?

A) Identifying the target audience

B) Setting the advertising objective

C) Determining the budget

D) Creating the advertisements

54

Mr. Hill's company typically charges his products $20 per unit with a profit margin of 25%. Eventually, the selling price decreased to $15 per unit but his company's current inventory consists of 200 units purchased at $16 per unit and the replacement cost also decreased to $13 per unit.

Which of the following is the exact value of inventory in the current market?

A) $3,000

B) $2,700

C) $2,600

D) $2,550

55

Cost-based pricing is the easiest way to calculate how a product should be priced. It involves estimating the cost of the product and then adding a percentage markup to determine the price.

Which of the following options is an example of cost-based pricing?

A) Basing the price on the features and benefits of the product.

B) Basing the price on what the customer is willing to pay.

C) Basing the price on the psychological expectations of the customer.

D) Basing the price on the full cost of production plus the required profit.

56

Crowdsourcing involves individuals or organizations obtaining needed services or ideas from a large number of people either paid or unpaid.

Which of the following would be the primary reason for using crowdsourcing in a company?

A) Product development

B) Sales promotions

C) Brand recognition

D) Market penetration

57

Forecasting is determining the direction of the future trends with the use of historical data.

Which of the following is the importance of forecasting in sales management process in companies?

A) It identifies the optimal time for the launch of a new product.

B) To analyze past sales of the products.

C) To gather employee opinion regarding company performance over the past years.

D) To estimate employee compensation for the upcoming year.

58

Management styles consist of different methods by which managers employ on making decisions, and relating to subordinates. This may depend on the type of business.

For example, a thousand cheese breads have been ordered into Julie's Bakery and to be picked up in three days. Mr. Arnold, the manager, sets the instructions without further suggestions or discussion with the employees.

Which of the following is Mr. Arnold's management style?

A) Participative

B) Autocratic

C) Laissez-faire

D) Democratic

59

The income acquired from the difference between sales of goods and services, and the cost due to returned or undeliverable merchandise is called the **sales revenue**.

Which of the following types of research is best to be used by a company if it wants to understand the effect of advertising spending on sales revenue?

A) Qualitative research

B) Descriptive research

C) Causal research

D) Exploratory research

CONTINUE ▶

## 60

Deferral means to delay recognizing certain revenues or expenses on the income statement until a later and more appropriate time.

Which of the following is an example of a deferral?

A) Accruing year-end wages

B) Recording prepaid rent

C) Recognizing revenues earned but not yet recorded

D) Recognizing expense incurred but not yet recorded

Retail traffic or **store traffic** is an important indicator of shopper behavior and a bellwether for retail sales results.

Which of the following would effectively increase a restaurant's store traffic by publicizing an opinion article about healthy food choices?

A) Posting the article on a public blog about local restaurants.

B) Displaying the article in the restaurant.

C) Publishing the article on the restaurant's website.

D) E-mailing the article to current restaurant customers.

This type of test is specially constructed to help predict how successful an individual is most likely to be in learning new skills.

What type of test is explained above?

A) Interest test

B) Aptitude test

C) Personality test

D) Achievement test

An **annual report** is a required document in corporate legislation, composed of a complete report of the audited accounts of a firm as well as its activities for the preceding year.

What section of an annual report would a financial statement reader find out if the financial statements of the company provided a fair depiction of its financial position and operating results?

A) Auditor's report

B) Balance sheet

C) Notes to the financial statement

D) Management discussion and analysis section

Ergonomics is defined as the design of an object made to minimize physical discomfort, especially for things used in the workplace.

Which of the following academic disciplines should be integrated into a discussion about the benefits of an ergonomically correct keyboard design?

A) Science
B) Social Studies
C) Language Arts
D) Mathematics

## 65

Net present value is obtained by getting the value of the present value of cash inflows minus the present value of cash outflows.

In which of the following circumstances will the net present value become negative?

A) The present value of cash outflows is higher than the present value of cash inflows.
B) The present value of cash outflows is higher than the present value of cash outflows.
C) The current value of cash inflows is higher than the present value of cash outflows.
D) The future value of cash inflows is higher than the present value of cash inflows.

## 66

Accounting involves a systematic and comprehensive recording of a business' financial transactions, as well as analyzing, summarizing, and reporting of these transactions to tax collection entities.

Which of the following are the forms of accounting?

A) Financial and structural
B) Managerial and equity
C) Managerial and financial
D) Statement and financial

A trade discount involves lowering of a product's published price.

Which of the following illustrates trade discount best?

A) In exchange for a used car, a discount is offered to the customer by the car dealer.
B) A homeowner is offered a discount by the lumberyard for purchasing lumber.
C) Retailers are offered a discount by a producer for its promotion of their product for a specific time.
D) Upon purchasing out-of-season merchandise, a retailer offered a discount to the buyer.

A variety of **pricing strategies** are used by businesses when selling products or services. These strategies involve setting the price aimed to maximize profitability for each unit sold or from the market overall.

Which of the following is the best pricing approach for the store owner of an ice-cream store with its old-fashioned, hand-cranked method of production?

A) Use of inelastic demand to price the product.

B) Use of status quo pricing to meet the competition.

C) Pricing the product based on the consumer's perceived value.

D) Pricing the product as cheaply as possible.

## 69

Which of the statements given below best describes a deferred income tax liability?

A) It is a contingent liability.

B) It can result in a deferred income tax asset.

C) It is recorded whether or not the difference between taxable income and financial accounting income is permanent or temporary.

D) It denotes the income tax payments deferred until future years due to the temporary differences between GAAP rules and tax accounting rules.

## 70

A **profit** is a financial gain obtained when the generated amount of revenue is higher than the expenses and taxes needed for sustaining a business operation.

Which of the following refers to the profit that is distributed to shareholders from the portion of a company's profit?

A) Earned income

B) Preferred stock

C) Dividends

D) Investments

Salespeople at a large consumer goods manufacturer were encouraged to design a presentation aimed to resent how their product will satisfy the wants of the customers. To do this, the salespeople ask questions to customers to identify their interests and desires then include them in the presentation.

Which of the following is the best presentation format represented in this scenario?

A) Stimulus-response format

B) Hard selling format

C) Need-satisfaction format

D) Formula selling format

72

Which of the following is responsible for enhancing the consumer experience by preparing the content and layout of a website including music clips, team photos, fan photos, testimonials, and other features?

A) A designer

B) A systems analyst

C) A copywriter

D) A brand manager

73

One type of demand elasticity is the **inelastic demand** which illustrates the extent of change in demand when there is a drop in price.

When does inelastic demand occur?

A) When the demand curve and the supply curve meet at a given price point.

B) When the quantity demanded changes barely with a difference in the price.

C) When the quantity demanded changes largely as prices change.

D) When the change in quantity demanded is in the same proportion as the price change.

74

Which of the following is a company engaged in when it builds its sales message, advertising message, and promotion aimed to influence how a particular market perceives their goods or services as compared to the competitors?

A) Mass customization

B) Concentrated targeting

C) Segmentation

D) Positioning

75

Which of the following is correct about marketing and business plans?

A) The focus of a business plan is in specific areas of the business, like marketing activities and product pricing, while the focus of a marketing plan is on the business as a whole.

B) A business and a marketing plan are the same and can be used interchangeably when discussing the business.

C) The focus of a marketing plan is on employment, chain of command, and a company's mission statement, while a business plan focuses on sales and advertising.

D) The business plan focuses on the business as a whole, including items such as the mission statement and financial plan, and the marketing plan focuses specifically on all marketing activities.

76

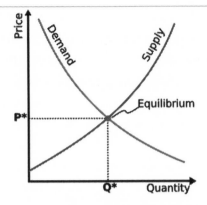

Based on the picture showing the supply and demand curves for leather garments, which of the following will occur in the market if the government places a price ceiling on leather garments below the equilibrium price?

A) There will be a shortage.
B) There will be a surplus.
C) The supply curve will shift rightward.
D) The demand curve will shift leftward.

77

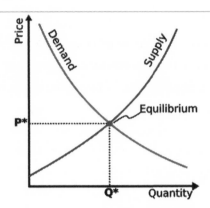

Based on the picture showing the supply and demand curves for leather garments, which of the following would be the effect of an increase in the price of leather and an increase in consumers' incomes on the equilibrium price and quantity of leather garments?

A) It would not be possible to determine the effect on the equilibrium price, but there would be a decrease in the number of leather garments.
B) The equilibrium price would increase, but it would not be possible to determine the effect on the number of leather garments.
C) Both the equilibrium price and quantity of leather garments decrease.
D) Both equilibrium price and quantity of leather garments increase.

133

CONTINUE ▶

78

Value Consciousness is used to measure a consumer's expressed tendency to buy products perceived to be of good value or worth.

Which of the following errors can be found in offering designer handbags in a company that targets value-conscious customers?

A) Basic stock list

B) Product mix

C) Enterprise resource planning

D) Open-to-buy policy

79

Micromarketing is a marketing strategy where the marketing or advertising efforts are focused on a small group of tightly targeted consumers.

Which of the following potential buyers is this strategy directed at?

A) Buyers who have opted out of customized marketing.

B) Buyers who have excess disposable income.

C) Buyers who share similar attitudes and behaviors

D) Buyers who are between the ages of 8 and 14

80

The **promotional mix** is one of the four elements that make up a marketing plan focused on a target market. It is also composed up of other components used as tools to communicate with the target market.

Which of the following elements of a promotional mix is responsible for handling unfavorable events?

A) Direct marketing

B) Personal selling

C) Sales promotion

D) Public relations

SECTION 7 MARKETING & ACCOUNTING

#	Answer	Topic	Subtopic	#	Answer	Topic	Subtopic	#	Answer	Topic	Subtopic	#	Answer	Topic	Subtopic
1	C	TB	S5	21	B	TB	S5	41	D	TB	S5	61	A	TB	S5
2	C	TB	S4	22	C	TB	S5	42	D	TB	S5	62	B	TB	S5
3	C	TB	S5	23	C	TB	S5	43	C	TB	S4	63	A	TB	S4
4	C	TB	S5	24	D	TB	S5	44	B	TB	S5	64	A	TB	S5
5	D	TB	S5	25	B	TB	S4	45	B	TB	S5	65	A	TB	S4
6	B	TB	S4	26	C	TB	S5	46	D	TB	S4	66	C	TB	S5
7	D	TB	S5	27	C	TB	S4	47	A	TB	S4	67	C	TB	S5
8	B	TB	S4	28	C	TB	S4	48	B	TB	S5	68	C	TB	S5
9	D	TB	S5	29	D	TB	S4	49	A	TB	S4	69	D	TB	S4
10	A	TB	S5	30	A	TB	S4	50	D	TB	S4	70	C	TB	S5
11	A	TB	S4	31	A	TB	S5	51	B	TB	S5	71	C	TB	S5
12	B	TB	S5	32	A	TB	S4	52	B	TB	S5	72	A	TB	S5
13	A	TB	S4	33	A	TB	S4	53	A	TB	S5	73	B	TB	S5
14	D	TB	S4	34	B	TB	S4	54	C	TB	S4	74	D	TB	S5
15	B	TB	S4	35	B	TB	S4	55	D	TB	S5	75	D	TB	S5
16	B	TB	S5	36	A	TB	S5	56	A	TB	S5	76	A	TB	S5
17	D	TB	S4	37	D	TB	S4	57	B	TB	S5	77	B	TB	S5
18	C	TB	S5	38	C	TB	S4	58	B	TB	S5	78	B	TB	S5
19	A	TB	S5	39	C	TB	S5	59	C	TB	S5	79	C	TB	S5
20	A	TB	S4	40	A	TB	S5	60	B	TB	S4	80	D	TB	S5

Topics & Subtopics

Code	Description	Code	Description
SB4	Accounting	TB	Business Basics
SB5	Marketing		

135

CONTINUE ▶

Made in United States
Orlando, FL
27 February 2023

30463519R00083